Patrick Augustine Sheehan

Geoffrey Austin

Student

Patrick Augustine Sheehan

Geoffrey Austin
Student

ISBN/EAN: 9783337214586

Printed in Europe, USA, Canada, Australia, Japan

Cover: Foto ©Thomas Meinert / pixelio.de

More available books at **www.hansebooks.com**

GEOFFREY AUSTIN
STUDENT

GEOFFREY AUSTIN
STUDENT

BY

CANON SHEEHAN, D.D.

Author of
"My New Curate" "The Triumph of Failure" "Glenanaar" "Lisheen"
"Luke Delmege" "Under the Cedars and the Stars" etc.

Alas! what are we doing all our lives, both as a necessity and as a
duty, but unlearning the world's poetry, and attaining to its prose?
This is our education as boys, and as men, in the action of life, in the
closet or the library, in our affections, in our aims, in our hopes, and
in our memories. — CARDINAL NEWMAN

τὸν φρονεῖν βροτοὺς ὁδώσαντα, τῷ πάθει μάθος
θέντα κυρ,΄ ς ἔχειν,
στάζει δ' ἐν θ' ὕπνῳ πρὸ καρδίας
μνησικήμων πόνος, καὶ παρ' ἄκοντας ἦλθε σωφρονεῖν

Agamemnon, 170-173.

Who guideth mortals into the way of being wise,
Who causeth them signally to have instruction by affliction,
But grief from the recollection of ills
Drops even in sleep over the heart,
And prudence comes even to the unwilling

Dublin
M. H. GILL AND SON, LTD.

PRINTED AND BOUND IN IRELAND
— BY —
M. H. GILL & SON, LTD., DUBLIN

CONTENTS

GEOFFREY AUSTIN: STUDENT

CHAPTER I

MY GUARDIAN

"O, wenn das Herz euch warnt, folgt seinem Triebe!
   Das Herz ist Gottes Stimme."
                                        SCHILLER.
'If your heart speak to you, follow its impulse.
   'Tis the voice of God."

I WAS just seventeen years old.

I had spent the last five years of my life in our diocesan seminary, where I learned to play handball well, and to become an excellent batsman, not to speak of knowing fairly Arnold's *Latin Prose Composition*, and Henry's *First Greek Book*; and I think I could have translated Virgil or Xenophon very well, if I had a good edition with copious notes, like Faussett's. Hitherto I had not dreamed of choosing a profession or other calling in life, to secure the wherewithal to live respectably. Life for me was a something to be enjoyed—not to be preserved. I had health enough to laugh at sickness and that mental ailment called ambition. I had a guardian, however, who thought it high time for me to lay my plans for the future; and towards the end of August 18—, at one of my frequent visits, and immediately after dinner, he introduced the subject. I must here say, that if ever man passed through life with all his best instincts unimpaired, his

I

spirits undepressed, and his heart unhardened, it was my guardian. There was a perpetual conflict going on between his head and heart. The one was exceedingly clear, the other was exceedingly soft and affectionate; and, like most soft things in this world, it generally gained the victory. In the matter of charity, for example, he would make the most frantic resolutions to be thrifty and economical, for he had a most decided propensity to get into debt; but the most transparent case of pretended poverty deceived him, and then, while his housekeeper raged, he had a philosophical way of consoling himself by the words of Pascal, of whom he was a great admirer: "Le cœur a ses raisons, que la raison ne connait pas." Something like the following scene was enacted night after night at his little presbytery. Hannah enters, dark and threatening.

"A woman at the door says she wants to see you, sir."

"Hannah," says Father Tom sternly, "what have I told you about these calls?"

"Very well, your Reverence, I'll send her away."

"Certainly, Hannah; I don't see what these people come here for at such an hour."

We would then resume our conversation, but I could see clearly that the mind of the old man was anxious and disturbed. Presently he would ring for Hannah. And Hannah would come in, muttering, "I thought so."

"Is that poor woman gone, Hannah?"

"No, sir."

"Ahem! What did she say exactly was her case?" This in a most judicial and critical manner, as if he had not the slightest idea of entertaining it if it were not a case of the clearest necessity.

"She says her husband had his arm whipped off by a threshing-machine at four o'clock to-day, and that he is gone into hospital, and they must amplicate it to-morrow."

"God bless me! you don't say so, Hannah! Here,

give the poor woman this, and tell her that I'll go to the hospital myself to-morrow and be present at the operation. I have a taste for these scientific experiments." This to me, who knew he would much rather suffer the amputation himself than witness it in another.

It was much the same feeling that made him the poorest preacher, although perhaps he was the most finished scholar, in his diocese. He had an idea that the poorest woman in his parish was infinitely better than himself; and he used to blush and be confused on Sundays, when he had to face his congregation and tell them those positive truths that seem too great to be uttered except by the lips of the All-Perfect. Believing himself to be very imperfect, he could not preach perfection to others, and his sermons, therefore, wanted that tone of conviction and self-confident dogmatism that impress susceptible audiences. Yet never have I known one possessed of such fine and accurate tastes. He had a splendid knowledge of the Classics (as I knew to my cost), especially of Horace, which he knew almost as well as his Breviary; and next after Horace, and probably owing to his French education, the greatest pleasure in his life was reading and analysing Pascal's *Thoughts.*

"Well, Geoffrey," he said to me this afternoon, "vacation is coming to a close."

"'Tis, sir," said I; "but I hope I am not going back to St. S——'s."

"No, indeed," said he slowly; "I have been thinking that we must make a change. You said, I think, that you didn't like the professions. Let me see. You objected to the priesthood because you didn't consider yourself worthy, nor do you think you ever will be. If you think so, my boy, I shall not force your wishes there. But what objection have you to become a doctor?"

"Well, sir," said I, with the dogmatic manner I had picked up in our Debating Society, "theoretically, none.

I admire the profession, perhaps I should say vocation, as such. But, practically, I don't understand making money out of the anguish and pain caused by the bodily infirmities of men."

" Whew !" said Father Tom, in surprise; "you're made, I see, for the Bar !"

"Certainly not, Father Tom," said I. "Whatever objections I have to living by the miseries of others, I have ten times a greater objection to march to fame or fortune over the bleeding hearts and blighted prospects of ninety per cent. of those who are lawyers' clients."

Anyone else would have called me a young prig; but Father Tom looked at me long and earnestly. Then he said gravely—

"I don't know, Geoffrey, where you have learned to speak in this manner. Young lads didn't speak so in my time. But whatever be thought of your language, your ideas are not too far wrong. I won't say that the professions are degraded; but there is some decided deordination in them. But keep, my boy, these ideas of humanity alive in your soul   You will have experiences enough to make you abandon them. The selfishness of men will harden you against men ; and the deceit of the world will make you think sometimes that men are made to serve as victims or tools for those who are clever enough to use them. But, my boy," said he earnestly, " never abandon yourself to bitterness or cynicism against your fellows. Christianity is the deepest and divinest knowledge of this world and of eternity, and it bears one word for ever emblazoned on its banners—Charity." It was on my lips to say something. " But," he continued, after a pause, " to be practical, there is only one other avenue to success open to you ; and that is the Civil Service. I understand that some valuable offices are open to competition. There is, for example, the Indian Service, where men, I am told, make money rapidly —I hope, honestly. Then there is the Sub-Inspectorship of Police—but I don't care for that, so long as English power uses its forces against the people. Then there is the Revenue Department, or, best of all, the Control Department in the Army. What do you think of that? An officer's uniform—gold lace from head to heel, epaulettes and stripes, and a good sword by your side "—

" And no fighting, Father Tom ? " said I.

" No," said my guardian; " you feed, the others fight."

" Hardly the thing for an Irishman," said I; " but I prefer it to any of your other fancy pictures."

" Well, be it so," said Father Tom; " and I'll look up in Dublin for a tutor. I should certainly prefer that you could reside in a college or academy, where you would be safe from the contamination of city life—but we'll do the best we can."

So the matter rested for some days; my boyish fancy being meantime very busy with dreams of a certain officer, very tall and distinguished, with uniform cut mathematically to the figure; and I dreamt of war and all its dread panoply, and the clanging of swords and the jingling of spurs were the music of my dreams.

Then one day a note came from Father Tom; and he met me in a state of great delight.

" Just the thing, Geoffrey," said he, " that I desired. I've had a letter this morning, and a prospectus of a new college opened in Dublin, and conducted nearly altogether on the tutorial or grinding system. A very dear old classfellow of mine, Father Bellamy, is rector; and he has a distinguished young graduate as vice-principal, and Latin, German. French, and mathematical tutors—just the place for you."

" Yes, sir," said I; " it seems to be exactly what we desire."

" I have ascertained," said he, " that with your attainments [here I winced] you can easily pass for the Control in twelve months. You will then be eighteen, and just eligible."

"And when must I leave, sir?" said I.

"Well," said Father Tom, "I won't press you, Geoffrey; but you know the value of time."

"Very well, sir," said I, " I shall be ready to start on Monday." This was Friday.

"Then come up and dine with me on Sunday," said he, looking pleased, "and we'll talk the situation over."

Sunday came, and we dined together; and, strange enough, almost for the first time in my life I felt exceedingly dispirited. I had been orphaned in my infancy, and my dying mother had placed me under the guardianship of this good priest. And so, with the exception of my college chums, I had grown up without giving or receiving much love from my fellow-creatures. And a young lad, with good health and spirits, does not generally take to brooding over his sad fate in life. It never occurred to me, therefore, to think my lot was cast in rough places in this world, because I did not receive those soft caresses or little tokens of love which were shared by my college companions. To tell the truth, I thought lightly of such things, especially as I saw how little they were appreciated by those who received them. Indeed, I was often not a little shocked at hearing our young lads speaking of their parents as " the Gov." and " the old woman "; and once I could have heartily licked a young scamp of my acquaintance, who was visited by his sisters—two pale girls in mourning after their mother's death. I saw them tear themselves away, their eyes swollen, as they said "good-bye" to this graceless puppy, and he sauntered up to the group where I was standing, and stopped his whistling for a moment to say, "I don't know what girls want in a place like this."

I usually spent my vacations at a distant watering-place which I was in the habit of visiting since I was a child. I loved every stone in its pebbly beach; and my heart used to swell with emotion as I stepped every summer from the railway carriage, and the "murmurs

and scents of the infinite sea" came to me. One
picture was for ever coming before me, the phantom of a
delight that can be tasted but once in life; and if ever
I walked alone on this beach it rose before me, to my
torture and delight. A glorious sunset, sky wrapped in
gold and purple, sea flashing back with dulled splendour
the glories of the sky. Deep peace and calm on all
things, but for the purring of the waves. A solitary
cottage on this very beach, with cliffs of sand rising
behind it. My mother walking here, my sister and I
gamboling and laughing as we ran towards, or fled
from, the approaching tide. Half the picture is here
still, for ever reproducing itself with the wanton kindness of Nature—sea and sky are here, with their music,
and splendours, and peace as of yore; but cottage and
cliff, mother and sister, have been blotted out, and with
them the infinite exuberance of youth, and the celestial
bliss of loving and being loved.

And so my affections, such as they were, were centred
on this good and guileless man, to whom my mother had
confided my future interests. I remember well the first
time I saw him. I was a mere child, and was standing
at a window overlooking the main street of our town,
when a strange procession passed by. A few loads of
hay and straw and turf, one solitary cart piled with
rough furniture such as a labourer might have, and the
priest trudging along the pavement, his aged mother on
one side, and his orphaned niece on the other, holding
his hand, as he proceeded from one scene of wretched-
ness to another—from the barren solitude of a mountain
at one end of the diocese, for ever wrapped in mists, and
black and stubborn even in summer, when the fields were
laughing with their harvests, and the trees were gay in
their feathery robes, to a dismal swamp where two of his
predecessors had perished from the vapours and slime
that dropped from the clouds above and sweated from
the marshes below. Child as I was, I understood the
significance of the sacrifice this man of God was making;
and the reverence begotten then bloomed and budded

into strong affection when I heard his voice, and knew the pressure of his hand.

But to resume. I felt very despondent this evening. After some vain attempts to rally me, Father Tom suggested a walk, and we strolled along the roads, where the first red leaves were whispering to the fall, until he led me to the little cemetery which surrounded his parish church. Now, if Father Tom had any failing at all, which I doubt, it was a pardonable pride in the manner in which this little cemetery was kept. He had an almost superstitious reverence for the dead. He knew every text on Death and Immortality that was spoken by pagan philosopher or Christian saint from Plato to Wordsworth; and he told me that whenever he came into God's Acre, as he called it, he had taught himself to see, not the plots of grass so carefully kept, nor the iron railings, nor the crosses or more ambitious ornaments over the graves : but he saw, robed in their white shrouds, with their still faces turned to the East, and the peace of Eternity on their eyelids, the undecayed and perfect bodies of the just that slept there. But he was scrupulously solicitous about the appearance of that cemetery. The walks were perfect, not a blade of grass showing in the gravel. The grass was kept mown down to the brown earth. Not a yellow weed, nor even an innocent daisy, was to be seen. The railings or chains had to be painted every year, and the lettering restored ; and if a lichen the size of sixpence appeared on limestone slab or marble cross, there was an immediate message to the person interested, who promptly removed the stain. We strolled along from grave to grave, and he told me the story of the occupants of each, and he vied with the epitaphs in charitableness, until at last we came to the spot where my own father and mother and sisters were laid. We knelt and prayed together. Then, as I rose, he pressed his hand on my shoulder, that I might remain kneeling. Then he said, and it was dreadfully solemn—

" Next after the sanctuary and the Holy of Holies, I

know no place more sacred than this. You are kneeling near the sleeping forms of those who gave you life, and were linked with you in that love which perishes not nor decays. I make no doubt they are watching you now; and if anything disturbs their eternal peace, it is their anxiety about the years that are speeding towards you, and which will be yours to make or mar—for better, for worse. But one thing I ask you to promise me in their presence: you will never let a morning pass without placing yourself in the presence of God. Do you promise?"

"I promise."

"You will never lie down to rest without reciting the Rosary of our Blessed Mother?"

"I promise."

I rose from my knees as the knights rose at the presence of their phantom king, and we went home. And as we went, he said many things to me which I had never heard before; and the mysteries of Life and Immortality were made very plain to me, in lessons which have been as a staff to the hand and as bread in the wilderness to the weary.

As I was about to say "good-bye," he went to his little escritoire, and took out five notes.

"Geoffrey," said he, "you know I'm not rich"—I thought of the turf and the straw—"but you'll want many things in college; and I won't touch your money, except to pay the £80 pension. You will then have one hundred and fifty left to buy a uniform. Then you'll want books and many other things, and a lad has more courage when he has a pound in his pocket."

"Father Tom," said I, "I will not—I cannot take it."

"Oh, but I insist."

"Oh, but I insist."

After a war of words, in which I was almost getting angry, I consented to take one pound. He folded the other notes regretfully, and said—

"Good-bye! Write often, and particularly if you are in trouble. You know you have no one but me"—

I turned away without a word, because there came
into my throat a curious swelling—that strange emotion
which, perhaps, does us more honour than the heavings
of vain ambition, or the pantings of foolish desire.

CHAPTER II

MAYFIELD

' A brow cut deep as with a knife
With many a dubious deed in life,
A brow of blended pride and pain
And yearnings for what should have been."

JOACQUIN MILLER.

I SUPPOSE there is something exhilarating in the speed
and variety of a railway journey, for I had hardly
stowed away my valise and coat next morning, as I
stepped into the mail for Dublin, when up went my
mood from the zero of despondency to the highest
degree of boyish animal spirits. I studied with unconscious intentness my fellow-travellers; I watched
the long ditches come sweeping into line, and the slow
procession of distant forests; I counted the telegraph
poles that dipped or rose with the road levels—all the
time my fancy singing some song to the rattle and roar
of the train, as we leaped and bounded and were flung
from side to side by the awful velocity. Since then I
have heard people say that engineers come to believe
that the giant power they direct is a living thing, that
must be petted and soothed and caressed, and that it
has peculiarities, vicious and otherwise, like a spirited
horse, and seems to know what is expected in a crisis,
and nerves itself to the wishes of its master, and seems
to know, when it glides into a station, whether it has
done well or ill. I can readily believe it; for I never
enter a railway carriage without the conviction that I
am committing myself to the mercies of a giant, who

probably will take me safely to my destination, but who may, in a fit of passion, if too much pressed, leap with me and all its freight into a ruin which fancy does not care to contemplate.

It was just at the close of the Franco-Prussian war, or rather that terrible sequel to it—the civil war between the Versaillais and the Commune; and the sympathies of Ireland, which were given so warmly to the "grande nation" in her distress, were still alive, but quivering with sorrow and indignation. Curious tales of the feelings of the lower classes in our cities and towns were related—tales of self-sacrifice and devotion to an ideal cause, which are not infrequent in the annals of our race. Partly for fun, and partly as an experiment, I determined to test the truth of these reports.

When I stood on the platform of the Kingsbridge terminus, I challenged the driver of a cab in execrable French as follows:—

"Voulez-vous m'apporter a college qu'on nomme 'Mayfield'?"

In an incredibly short time a crowd had gathered; and whilst poor cabby was looking into the crown of his hat in his perplexity, he was mercilessly assailed by the bystanders.

"Yerra, Jim, why don't you spake to the gintleman? Sure, you haven't forgotten your French, man, since you wor in college?" "Say it again, sor," said a young gamin, whose attire was more airy than respectable; "it's some time since he was in France, and you must spake aisier." And some, whispering amongst themselves, came rapidly to the conclusion, "A young gentleman escaped from the siege of Paris!"

I tried again, this time in bad English.

"I wish you to me carry to a house which they call 'Mayfield.'"

"Mayfield! Mayfield! Where the devil is that?" said the cabman.

"Sure 'tis the Twelve Acres in the Phœnix Park be

manes," said another driver; "drive him round the
Park, Jim, and set him down at the Impayrial."

Jim was going to act on that suggestion, when I
interposed, again in broken English—

" The house is in some place where the Irish do break
the heads at the Fair."

"Donnybrook! be gobs!" said they all in chorus;
and with three times three for France we set out on our
journey. I need hardly say that I was silent; but my
companion made up for it by nods and winks, and hinted
sometimes in more articulate language, that he was
carrying a most distinguished personage. Whenever a
block occurred on the quays or streets, the drivers of
less honoured vehicles, and the conductors of the tram-
cars, were informed of my nationality, my past history,
and my future prospects The first of these never
changed; but the two latter particulars grew and
developed in majesty and importance as we proceeded.
I heard Jim tell a fellow-driver at the corner of Sackville Street that I had just escaped from the siege of
Paris; at the corner of Grafton Street, that I was
"a young ossifer come over to learn ingineering in
Ireland"; at the eastern end of Stephen's Green, I was
"the fust to inter Paris after the blagard Communists
were expelled"; and lastly, when we had got into the
suburbs, and imagination was free to revel as it chose,
" I was sint specially by MacMahon to steady the fortifications of Dublin Harbour; and we know the rest."

And so, half amused with my conductor, half curious
about my destination, we turned sharply to the right
from the Donnybrook road, rattled up a short byway,
and came to an exceedingly shabby lodge, whitewashed
and unplastered. The gates were opened by an old
woman, and, after a semicircular drive around an ill-
kept lawn, we drew up at the door of the college. I
had then to face the unpleasant task of undeceiving my
imaginative driver.

"Combien faut-il payer?" I said. " How much shall
I pay?"

"Nothing, sir," said he gallantly. "Nothing to a Frenchman. I'd do more than that for your country."

"But," said I, speaking in my natural tone of voice, "I am not a Frenchman."

"W—what ?" said he, starting back in surprise.

"I am not a Frenchman," I repeated ; "I was never in Paris in my life, so I couldn't have escaped ; I was never even a private in the Army, much less an officer ; I didn't enter Paris with Trochu, and never had the pleasure of knowing him ; and I have not been sent by MacMahon or anyone else to study fortifications. All the same, you are a good fellow, and here's your fare, and something with it. Now, help me with this trunk."

He stood during this explanation like one suddenly paralysed, his mouth open, his whip lying carelessly in his hands. Then he heaved a bitter sigh, as he thought how his splendid fabric was rudely knocked to pieces, and how he dare not tell at the public-house that night all that ho had been inventing, when the very foundations of his story had been uprooted. But he simply said, in a tone of bitter regret, "God forgive you, sir !"

He turned away mournfully, adjusted the harness, and his anger outbidding his sorrow, he changed his whole tone.

"Be gobs, what a play-boy you are! All the way from the bogs of Kerry to make fools of dacent people! It's on the boords of the Gaiety, or perhaps the Theayter-Royal, we'll soon see you, unless you are transported for swindling."

He bit the coin I gave him, lest there might be deception even there ; and, seeing that I was not inclined to answer him back, he gave a saucy blow to his horse, and cantered down the avenue. Once or twice I saw him look back with his mouth screwed up, and he shook his head mournfully, as if to predict an evil future for me.

Mayfield was to all outer appearance a splendid

mansion. Two rather shortened wings, the entire width
and height of which were occupied with broad, stately
windows, were thrown out at its sides; and, in the
centre, a long, broad flight of limestone steps led up to
a portico, whose rounded pillars upheld a pediment,
crowned by a reclining statue of some pagan goddess.
Evidently it was one of those stately buildings which
the enterprise and artistic tastes of Ireland threw up in
that short period in her history when the incubus of
foreign and hostile domination was lifted.   Up that
avenue rolled the carriages of her nobility, ancestral
and intellectual, to one of those Augustan entertain-
ments which were freely given at the time.   Thronging
those steps were the brilliant wits of Dublin, and the
officers of the Volunteers in their picturesque uniforms,
and orators, the echoes of whose words were vibrating
through the land, and stately ladies, who came to relieve
the heaviness of masculine humour by the brightness
and *esprit* that belong to intellectual beauty.   I was
not at all surprised when, in answer to the bell, I was
ushered into a stately hall, whose ceiling was loaded
with arabesques, and whose floor was covered with a
rich mosaic of tiles, of which we have lost the pattern
and the secret.   I allowed the servant to go on before
me with my trunk and valise, whilst in the twilight I
measured and studied and wondered, when a door shot
open at my left, and I heard—
    " What brought you here at study-time, sir ? "
    I turned, and saw one whom I took to be a professor
He was rather tall of stature, and with somewhat
rounded shoulders; and when he came near me in the
twilight, I saw that he was a decidedly intelligent-look-
ing man, with those large brown eyes that are frequently so brilliant in shortsighted people.   But there
was a fierce accent of contempt in his tone of voice that
made me feel uncomfortable,—a harsh, cold, grinding,
supercilious tone, that was never loud, but always
strident and contemptuous.
    " I have only just arrived by the mail, sir," said I

respectfully, as I studied for the first time the academical dress.

"Oh, a new pupil, I suppose?" said he.

I nodded.

"Where from?"

He spoke in a quick, snappish tone, that at any other time would have made me angry.

I told him.

"You are going to study for—?" he said inquiringly.

"The Control Department in the Army," I answered.

"Pah!" said he, "you've not the slightest chance of passing this year. Let me see," he continued, hiding his arms under his gown, and measuring me from head to foot, as if to gauge my mental endowments by my height and width in inches; "you know the First Book of Cæsar, Lucian's *Dialogues*, the First Book of Euclid —no French—no German—you never wrote a Latin sentence in your life—there will probably be twenty places for five hundred candidates—what in the world brought you here?"

I was so completely mystified, I couldn't answer, but he relieved me.

"Where are your letters?"

I took out the two that were written by my guardian to Father Bellamy—one private, the other containing a few lines from the president of the seminary where I had studied.

"I have been directed," I said, "to deliver these in person to Father Bellamy."

"I'll deliver them," he said, taking them from my hand, and deliberately breaking the seals. "By the way, have you had dinner?"

"No," I said angrily, for I thought this act of his quite dishonourable.

"Then," he cried, turning away to a window in the hall, "you had better see the housekeeper, get some dinner; you may then see your room, and go to studies; you can meet your tutors to-morrow."

As a new boy, I did as I was desired; but I took

away from that first interview an aversion to that man, which never after was quite mitigated.

After supper, as the evenings were still fine, the boys gathered on the steps in front of the portico, and I thought I should have to pass through some fiery ordeal, according to school traditions that are as old as the times of St. Basil and St. Gregory. But I was agreeably disappointed. Twenty boys were gathered on the steps; but they were the quietest, if not the dullest, lads I had ever seen. I thought at the time that it was the late partings from home that made them so spiritless; but I soon discovered that the shadow of a dread examination, even at the remote end of twelve months, was flinging itself backward over these young lives, and checking the exuberance and life which we always associate with the schoolboy. A few, too, had been plucked the previous summer, and this was their last chance; and all had the appearance of having become prematurely old. One lad alone reminded me that there was still a spring-time of life in this world.

"I say," said he, coming in front of me on the steps, his hands stuck deep in his pockets, and a general *sans souci* air about him, "ain't you rather a big fellow to come to such a place as this?"

"What's your name?" I said in reply, looking him straight between the eyes.

"That's nothing to you," he replied saucily; "you can call me Cal, like all the fellows here. But what brought you here?"

"Well, my Lilliputian friend," said I, "I am sent here specially by the Government to give a report of the educational working of this place, and especially of the progress of a young gentleman, whose intellect I am sure is somewhat greater than his stature."

For Cal was small, with round grey eyes, and black curls rolling over his forehead and blinding him.

He was called Cal, an abbreviation of Calendar, for he studied all things but his books, and knew all things but his lessons. The history of the mansion, some legend of a mighty crime committed there, when the Hell-Fire Club was rampant in the city, the names, dates of birth, and the profession of the parents of every student, and the history of every professor in the house, were perfectly well known to him.

"Can you play ball?" he asked, continuing his cross-examination.

"Yes."

"And cricket?"

"Yes."

"What else?"

"I can ride, swim, and shoot."

"I say, Travers, he'll lick all the fellows here, and yourself into the bargain."

I turned, and saw by my side a boy, whose head just reached my shoulder. A pale-faced boy, whose pallor, however, was no sign of delicacy. Soft, fair hair rippled across his forehead. He had big, blue-black eyes, and, as Cal spoke, a slight blush crossed his face and tinged his forehead.

"Oh, never mind me, Cal," he said quietly; "I am very glad someone has come with whom it is worth while to play."

"Well," said Cal patronisingly, "come with me, and I'll show you the place."

Nothing loth, I went with my new friend to see all that was interesting in my new home. He showed me the pigeon-house, where he and Charlie Travers and another boy kept their pigeons, and he called to one, that came to him with some difficulty, I thought, which was explained by the fact that he was blind; he showed me where a wild youth, named Somers, scaled the walls, and went to the city last winter on the occasion of some great political demonstration; he showed me the corner where Charlie Travers licked O'Dell, whom he said he detested; and, coming round the other side of the building, he pointed out as a *pièce de resistance* a large square building, just outside

2

our walls, but on a lower level, and cried, "And there's where the looneys live."

"Who are the looneys?" said I. "What are they re- markable for?"

"Don't you know?" he said. "Why, man, that's a private asylum. When I came here first, we used to have the greatest fun, shooting peas at the looneys, and making faces at them, when they came to the windows; and usedn't they be mad, shaking their fists at us, and tearing at the bars with their hands, and even with their teeth—till the Grinder heard it, and then the doctor took them away to the other end of the house, and shut up these rooms. But all the new boys used to be frightened out of their lives at night when they heard the howling and screaming of the mad people, and the shouts of the keepers, and—and the silence."

"Who is the Grinder?" I said, anxious to change the gloomy subject.

"Haven't you met him yet?" said he.

"No," said I; "the only person I have met as yet was a professor in a square hat and gown, who pulled me up for being out of study, as I arrived from the train."

"Was he near-sighted, and did he speak sharp?" queried Cal.

"Rather too sharply," said I, "for my tastes."

"That's the Grinder," said Cal, screwing up his mouth, and drawing in his breath; "you'll know him better by and by."

"But why is he called the 'Grinder'?" said I.

"Because he *is* a grinder," said Cal illogically.

"You mean he prepares boys for special examina- tions?" I said.

"Well, you *are* an innocent!" said Cal. "No," he continued; "but because, of all the bitter, cantankerous, sour-tempered men that ever lived, he is the worst. Because he grinds and gnashes his teeth when he is crossed, and particularly when he is flogging us, and he flogs us all but Coulette."

"Who is Coulette?"

"Coulette is a half nigger, half mulatto, half quadroon, half white, such as you might meet in Cooper's novels. He has short, crisp hair like a negro, black eyes that spit fire, the smallest hands and feet in the world, a big white sombrero, which he says is worth all the shoddy hats in Dublin, and which he gets washed once a year"—

"But why is he not flogged?" I interrupted.

"Because," said Cal, with infinite gusto, "the Grinder daren't look cross at him. He would fly at him like a panther. He was picked up by the rector somewhere away in New Orleans, and was brought here to be educated—God bless the mark! He is for ever cursing the climate, the food, the professors, but, above all, the Grinder."

"But didn't the Grinder ever try to tame and civilise this wild animal?" said I.

"He did," said Cal, with a smile, "he did. One day last year, during the Christmas holidays, Coulette was in the study-hall—his body sunk in an easy-chair, and his feet absolutely perpendicular, and resting on the stove. He was singing at the top of his voice—

'Fairy Bell!
She's my gentle Fairy Bell!
The star of the night, and the lily of the dell!
Fairy Bell!
She's my gentle Fairy Bell!
Long may she ramble on her bright majestic way!'

when in burst the Grinder! 'That's no posture for a gentleman to sit in,' said he. Coulette sprang up, collared him, and pushed him back against the wall, stuttering and stammering, for he has a frightful impediment. 'D-d-do you c-c-call yourself a gentleman?' said he. 'Do you? do you? do you?'— and at each question he knocked the Grinder's head against the wall. Then, taking him to the door, he pushed him into the corridor. Since then the Grinder lets Coulette alone. But he licks all the other fellows, and he'll lick you."

"Will he?" said I. "I am rather old for such a thing."

"You'll find he will," said Cal.

"We'll see," said I.

Words innocent enough, but which Cal construed into a defiance; and as such they were carried from ear to ear, until they reached the Grinder himself, who accordingly regarded me from the outset as a dangerous rebel.

"But who is the Grinder?" I asked again.

"That's what puzzles me," said Cal, in a comical tone of perplexity. "That's the only thing I can't make out. I have discovered that he is some relation, probably a nephew, of the rector's; and there is some story connected with his past life, which I cannot make out. But I will. He is an M.A. of Trinity, and has several other titles. But don't we hate him! There's the night-bell. Come along, or we'll catch it."

I thought we would have night prayers, as in the seminary; but no. We scampered upstairs to our rooms, and prayed or not, as we pleased. But I remembered my vow; and, after I had said my Rosary, I flung off my coat, and stood looking over at the grim building where the "looneys" were detained. Dead silence reigned through the house and all around. Not a light flashed in the asylum; but I thought of the restless brains that were pulsing and throbbing in the high fever of delirium beneath that roof, and the grim keepers moving from bed to bed during the lonesome watches of the night, and never relaxing their vigilance. Then I thought of the Grinder, and the singular dislike I had for the man; and I wondered would we ever get into conflict? Then my thoughts wandered to the boys whom I had seen, and all of whom, except Cal, appeared to be terrible duffers; and I made up my mind to take them coolly, and not to be too friendly with any of them, when I heard a tap at my door, so light that I waited to have it repeated. It was repeated. I opened the door, and a voice said—

"May I come in ?"

I closed the door softly, and the young lad who had spoken to me with Cal entered.

"My name is Charlie Travers," said he, as he sat on the edge of the bed. "I have come to say that I want to be friends with you. I like you, and so does Cal; and the three of us must be friends. I said at once, "All right, Charlie; why not ?" So we sat together and talked; and he told me of his home down in Clare, of his boating and fishing, of his mother and sister Mary, and how he was going in for the Indian Civil Service, and how awful hard the examination was. And we didn't mind the time passing, till the far-off clock in the city chimed the quarters and struck ten. Then Charlie said, "I must be off now. The Grinder may come round. Good-night !"

CHAPTER III

MY LATIN TUTOR

"Unwinding the cerements of antiquity, let us not be contaminated with their dust !"

THE system of education at Mayfield for the grown boys who were preparing for the Civil Service, or for the examinations preliminary to entering for the professions, was what is called tutorial. There were no classes. The students read in private, or in the large common study-hall; and they were helped by catechetical instructions or explanations by their tutors, whom they met at appointed hours. Accordingly, at ten o'clock the morning after I entered Mayfield, I was ushered into a small room or hall by the Grinder, and curtly introduced to Mr. Dowling, my Latin tutor. I thought there was a slight sneer in the manner in which the former said, "He has brought letters of recommendation from some good people down the country, and appears to have read a little: brush him up, Mr. Dowling, if only for our own sakes."

Mr. Dowling, as I looked at him then, was not exactly my ideal of a professor. Very tall and angular, but perfectly straight, he appeared to have got a military training; and there was a certain foppishness in his dress and air that betokened anything but the rapt devotee of learning. He had large soft eyes, that gave you the impression that he was shortsighted, and a profusion of fair beard curled around his lips and chin, and was carefully pointed, in what I understood was the style in the time of Charles I. My prejudices, however, if I can call them so, vanished as he came forward, the moment the Grinder had left, and shook my hand warmly, and said—

"I am very happy to know you, Mr. Austin. Now, as a preliminary, tell me all about yourself."

I have since then heard, and read very often, of excellent people using strong and splenetic language about voice and accent; and I have heard of the treason of exchanging the silvery and melodious brogue for an electro-plated English intonation. About that matter I should not care to offer an opinion, as accent is rather a relative than positive quality; but I do venture to say that if anyone had listened to these few words, spoken in the softest, quietest, distinctest tones, he would have awakened, as I did, to the perception that the voice is the most flexible and powerful organ of melody; and that language in its mere physical utterance is the highest of arts. I had never heard anything like this before. Vigorous and stirring speakers I had heard; and I had had experiences of voices against which I closed my ears. I had known the strident hiss of vulgar passion, and the painful mincing of affectation; but now, for the first time, I heard a trained and tranquil voice, that had been toned and softened like the strings of some delicate instrument, and I thought I saw each syllable that was pronounced, and the very shape of the letters. I told him my story simply; and if I had anything to conceal, I am sure that soft voice would have beguiled me into a confession. And then: "What had I studied?"

"A little Livy, a book of Homer, Lucian, and Xenophon."

" I don't mean what authors you have read," said he kindly; "but what have you learned?"

I looked puzzled.

" I beg your pardon," said he; "but what I am desirous of ascertaining is, what knowledge exactly you have acquired of the Greek and Latin languages. For example, have you ever written Latin?"

" No."

"Do you think you understand the construction of the language?"

"I think I understand most of its idioms," I said, "and the peculiar terms and expressions that are used, and the difference of the synonyms."

I blushed violently as I showed my little stock of wares under such high-sounding phrases.

"Ah!" he said cheerily, "you have brought the bricks, and very sound, square bricks they are. You and I will put a pretty handsome edifice together, I think."

I must have been very sensitive at this time, I believe, for just as my spirits went down into the abyss when I met the Grinder the evening before, they shot up now with surprising celerity. I warmed to the gentlemanly-looking man before me; and though animated with a certain fear, I thought I should like very much to make him my friend. The desire increased, as every day revealed his character more fully to me. I had made the acquaintance, I found, of a profound and enthusiastic student. He lived in his books, and these books were the ancient Classics. He no more belonged to our century, with its hard selfishness, its conceited superficiality, its hollow pretences, than the mummies over in the Academy. Through the medium of the ancient masterpieces which the monks saved for the world, he entered into that civilisation of which such few tangible relics remain. He habitually let his fancies wander away to the sunny skies of the south, the blue Mediterranean, the tideless Ægean studded with islets, the bright atmosphere, and the warm waters that had felt the sweep of the triremes; and he had filled in the picture with figures of dusky, supple Greeks, and brown, stately Romans, until he could call up at will the scenes of history and literature, and make a tableau of them as perfect as Alma Tadema ever painted, whilst here at hand were the very words they spoke, and the ear was enchanted with rhythmic Greek or sonorous Latin, whilst the eye of the imagination revelled in scenes of ravishing beauty over which the softened lights of distance and memory fell. The one hope of his life was to be able at some future, indefinable date to look with his eyes on those pictures which were already so familiar to him. No dark Mohammedan ever yearned to see the Mecca of his fathers so earnestly as my tutor yearned to see the Forum where Cicero addressed the *Patres Conscripti*, or the ruined theatres where, with no canopy but the blue sky of heaven, no scenery but the purple mountains in the background, and the "anerithmon gelasma" of the sea in front, Æschylus put his immortal tragedies on the stage. For Mr. Dowling had his favourite authors amongst the ancients. The Attic orators he scarcely used, although he might have read through them as easily as through a speech in the House of Commons; and Latin poets, always excepting Virgil, he held in a kind of disdain. But he revelled in the rich beauties of the Athenian tragedies, and was very happy with the Socratic dialogues, and the higher philosophies of Plato; but his patron saint was Cicero. It was no surprise to me, therefore, to learn that his only friends in the large city were a certain professor, who had spent his life in editing the Classics, and a Polish priest, who said mass every morning at a city hospital, and gave the rest of the day and night to study. Such men, who study for the sake of learning, without a single thought of ambition or reward, are scattered in large numbers around our city. They form a republic by themselves, although they may not be known to each other. They are seldom seen by day, except when flitting from store to store on the Dublin quays; but they will gather to a book auction, as birds of a dark night congregate around the light. To these strange denizens, priests of learning, a Greek accent is of more importance than an Act of Parliament; and the discovery of Aristotle's Constitution of Athens was a far more important event than the locating of Lake Nyanza or the discovery of the tributaries of the Nile.

Mr. Dowling's method of teaching was, to say the least, peculiar. His first act in the morning, when he put up his hat and overcoat, was to take the *Freeman's Journal* from his pocket, and, casting his eye over the leading articles or some Parliamentary speech of the night before, he would ask me to translate it into Latin. This was a sore task to me in the beginning; and what misgivings I had when I handed up my first exercise to him! But he neither smiled nor looked disappointed, though it must have tried him sadly.

"Very good, very good," he said deliberately. "Now, how would Cicero have put it?"

I am sure I could not imagine. But the question was not addressed to me. It was a soliloquy.

"Would you turn over to that oration, *Pro Lege Manilia?* Let me see—what edition have you? Yes. Now look at the fourth page of that oration. Read the sentence commencing " Majores vestri."

"Now, do you see any resemblance between that sentence and the one you have just written? I mean in the ideas?"

I did; but, Heaven help me, how differently put!

"Now, you notice how Cicero expresses that idea. Will you remember it?"

"I'll try."

And so, day by day, I began to see that my mind
was growing and developing under his genial and
kindly influence; and the laborious work of translating,
etc., was lightened by an enthusiasm such as I had
never felt before. For, like all boys, I had a most
thorough dislike to the hard, dry details of study; and,
let me say, my preceptors had hitherto done all they
could to make the labour doubly trying, from the dry,
mechanical way they pursued it. I had been working
in the dark. I had been making bricks without straw.
I neither knew nor cared to know the language whose
beauties I could not see. I was engaged in erecting
a mighty scaffold around a large building that was
obscured from me; and the ropes cut me and pained
me, till I fled from the work in horror. But my new
tutor commenced by showing me the building in all its
antique and massive magnificence, and then he bade me
learn the 'passwords and go within.

He excited an enthusiasm, a passion, which, after
the holy desires of religion, is the purest man can
experience. I would know how these ancients thought
and felt; what ideas they had formed of the mystery
of life; how they had studied the workings of the
human heart. Beneath these symbols and legends,
absurd and profane as they are, I would see some
meanings of the philosophy of life, its burdens and its
joys. There, in the dawnings of intellectual life, I
would trace the sublime impatience of disquieted minds
with this riddle of life, and the lofty conjectures of
great but darkened intellects at finding some clear way
out of the labyrinth where they groped in blindness.
And Æschylus and Euripides became friendly words
with me; and I dug out their treasures, which they
gave sparingly, with labour that was lightened by a
restless craving for knowledge. And if ever I flagged
or grew weary, my gentle monitor was nigh to stimulate
and encourage.

"I think, Mr. Dowling, that all this classical study is
labour in vain. I suppose I must go through it for my

examination. But what use will it be to me afterwards ?"

He looked at me in surprise the first time I showed a tendency to rebel against his doctrines. Afterwards, he grew accustomed to me. But sometimes, I am sorry to say, I put him quite out of temper; there would be a coolness between us for a few days, and then our old relations would be resumed. I remember one of these occasions, when I gave myself up to a regular fit of *dolce far niente*, and conceived a most violent dislike to these studies. After a few querulous remarks, I had the impertinence to say—

"But, Mr. Dowling, if all this be true, why didn't you do something for yourself in early life ? It seems to me that a man of your abilities ought not to content himself with a miserable living of a hundred a year, and a few tuitions."

Like a great many other things I have said during my life, I would have given worlds to recall these words as soon as they were uttered; for they threw my tutor into a state of great agitation. He paced up and down the room for a few minutes, nervously pulling his moustache, and then he stood opposite me, and tried to look calm, but he bit off his words as he spoke—

"And do you think that the Eternal and Omniscient gave poetry to the Greeks, and eloquence to the Romans, that you and I might eat bread as the result of their genius and labour ? Did Æschylus dream his divine dreams, and Cicero weave the spells of his undying eloquence, that a few wretched mortals in a far-off and barren century might earn a few sesterces more or less by interpreting them to the more stupid of their countrymen ? Or did they utter the sacred thoughts within them in the highest modes of their respective arts, because the Spirit seized them and dwelt in them, and spoke His inspirations through their lips ? And we who have had the good fortune to come after them, and to whose eyes are revealed the highest workings of human reason, and the highest

flights of human imagination, shall we be guilty of the
sacrilege of lifting ourselves on the low steps of human
ambition by a knowledge that was never intended to be
bought and sold ? Shall we exchange immortal thought
for the food and raiment that perish ? Shall we dig out
stones from the pyramids of kings, wherewith to build
our own wretched kraals?   Are the Classics, which
ought to be porticoes to the temples of the gods, to be
degraded into vulgar byways to Excise departments
and Custom House appointments?   In Heaven's name,
let people teach compound addition and the spider's
webs of mathematics to men whose lives will be spent
in totting up L. S. D., and calculating how many barrels
are in bond, and how much poison might safely be
scattered amongst men.   But why degrade the kings of
our race into vassals to help the golden youth of our
generation into positions which a Roman slave would
not occupy ? 'I have seen fools on horseback, and
kings walking in the mire.' So shall it be to the end,
O Preacher !"
     Then he laughed gently at his own impetuosity,
and we were as good friends as before. But many a
lecture I got from him afterwards on "plain living
and high thinking," owing to my one unlucky
remark.
     But there was one point on which he was inexorable,
and, indeed, unreasonable — his utter detestation of
mathematics.   And as that science entered largely into
my course of studies, it was the occasion of bringing
me into frequent friendly disputations with him. I say
friendly, because his anger was only what children call
"make - believe."   Principally from conviction and
reason, yet partly for fun, and partly to get an opportunity of saying outré and absurd, but clever things—
a habit of which he was very fond, and which was to
me a mighty attraction—he would open an argument,
and the moment I threw out a single idea that he could
safely catch, he would smile, rub his hands, and com-
mence a course of reasoning, ridicule, laughing, and

bantering, that was infinitely amusing, and not unin-
structive.

"I could not find time, Mr. Dowling, to get beyond
this chapter last night. I had to give some time to a
problem, which Mr. Ferris asked me to look up for
him."

"A problem? in what, sir?"

"A simple cut in Euclid, sir—I mean, simple enough
to those who understand such things, but very difficult
for me."

"And how much time, might I ask, did you give to
this difficult problem?"

"Well, I think I was racking my brains for two
hours over it, and was none the wiser."

"And supposing that you did solve it, sir, what
then?"

"Well, I think Mr. Ferris must be pleased."

"And what then?"

I was silent.

"And is it possible that Mr. Ferris could ask any
young man to spend two hours of valuable time in
poring over the mechanism of crooked lines and
battered circles. I have seen a black-board once or
twice in my life covered with hideous tattooing; and to
extend the simile, I have seen youths uttering a jargon
to which the inarticulate sounds of a South Sea
Islander would be a classic language. But why this
dreadful science is permitted in a course of liberal
education, I cannot for the life of me imagine! I can
admire the lines that shoot with precision through the
masts and yards of a man-of-war; but I know that
network of ropes serves some definite object. I can
admire the delicate curvings which I see in Nature, the
tender rounding of a rose-petal, or the sweep of an
ocean ridge, or the lines of a yacht towards its stem,
or the swelling of its sails as it goes curtseying over the
billows. But what has anyone to see or argue about
in lines that are irregular, and circles that are not
round, and a system of abstract reasoning that com-

mences with some postulate which everyone admits, and ends in a proposition which no one cares to deny, and which has not the slightest bearing on life or its issues?"

"But, sir, you know very well that the sciences and arts are wedded. The one are dependent on the other. You speak of the Forum! How was it built?"

"How was it built?—with brick and mortar, of course; or perhaps Sicilian marble."

"Yes; but how were these bricks laid?"

"One over the other, I presume!"

"At random, like the Tower of Babel?"

"I suppose not. I presume they were laid in lines of regularity and beauty."

"By means of certain principles?"

"I suppose so."

"And these principles were found in what science?"

"Look here, Mr. Austin, this Socratic reasoning won't do. Your science commences with a sophism: and if you lay your foundations on sand, where will your building be? A point has position, but not magnitude! Can you conceive it? A line is the progression of a point, which point, remember, is non-existent and impossible. A surface is the progression of a line, which is a series of points which have no magnitude. A cube is the progression of a surface which is made up of lines which have neither length nor breadth. This is pure idealism—the science of bubbles. It may do for dreamy, bibulous Germans; but how any man can turn from the luminous, logical pages of Cicero to find out that A B C is equal to D E F, I cannot imagine, unless on the general grounds of the darkness of intellect superinduced on our race by the iniquity of Adam. Listen!"

He would then read, in his fine, soft, sonorous voice, some superb passage from Cicero or Virgil, accentuating every syllable with the utmost precision up to the grand climax. Then, closing the book with a bang, and snapping his fingers, he would shout—

"What's your d——d A plus B to that?"

But one day he checked himself in the midst of a burst of enthusiasm, and, after a glorious eulogy of his masters, in which he exulted in such phrases as "the thunderous lilt of the Greek epic," "the marching-songs and marriage-songs of the world," "the dramas, in which gods only should be actors," etc., etc., he appeared for a moment lost in thought; then, laying his hand gently on my shoulder, he said—

"I have seen the passage somewhere—it matters not where; but it runs thus, and keep it in thy memory—

"'Unwinding the cerements of antiquity, let us not be contaminated with their dust!'"

CHAPTER IV

MONSIEUR LE COMTE

"Anyone watching keenly the stealthy convergence of human lots, sees a slow preparation of effects from one life on another, which tells like a calculated irony on the indifference, or the frozen stare, with which we look on our unintroduced neighbours."—G. ELIOT.

THE friendship so simply initiated between Charlie Travers, Cal (whose real name was Willy Sutton), and myself, grew stronger every day; and every day I was more grateful for it, as I looked around and began to understand clearly the circumstances of the place. I should be very sorry to leave on the minds of any readers who may have penetrated thus far in this "owre true tale," the impression that I was either very clever or very faultless. I was simply a fair average young lad, without much culture or education, but with a very strong desire to be successful in life; whilst, without much piety, I think I had some perception of the nobility of certain human excellences, and the baseness of certain perversities; and an attachment to and respect for religion which nothing could shake. I did not belong to the goody-goody school at all; but I was not a little pleased and flattered to think that the best elements in the college, in the shape of my new friends, came around me without any seeking on my part, and the worst kept away studiously from me, and regarded me with distrust. For here, under this little span of sky, the eternal conflict, too, was raging—the fight of the Standards that goes on through the world, in the tumult of mighty cities and the solitude of deserts, on the hills and in the valleys; amongst vast masses of population, where some great principle is struggling for existence against the cruelty and selfishness of men; and in the veiled silence of each solitary heart, where passion is raging, and the "still, small voice" trying to make itself heard above the tempest. I think I have already hinted that religion was not one of the departments in this academy of all the sciences. With examinations on which the reputation, and even the existence, of the college depended, looming up before professors and students, there was no time or thought for that department which did not enter into the examination programme. So each student was left to tend the little garden of his own soul as he pleased; and many ran to weeds in the experiment.

I have not yet said a word about the rector, Father Bellamy. He did not exist for us but in name. That name he lent, at special request, to his nephew, Hugh Bellamy, when the latter was establishing this school, and as it was known and respected in the ranks of the Irish priesthood, and even in that wider circle whose centre is a liberal education, it served its purpose well. But the rector had no more influence on the well-being or education of the boys than the Provost of Trinity College, or the President of the College of Surgeons. He had his apartments in a quiet corner of the house, where he laboured and studied with as much earnestness as if life and its prizes were still before him, instead of having been flung behind him in contempt. His library was well stocked, and, strange to say, very-

neat; and certain weird-looking batteries and retorts
gave one an idea that this was the home of some
mediæval scholar, who had not yet abandoned the
pursuit of magic stones and life-elixirs. Father
Bellamy had travelled—so I had learned from Cal—
and he still kept up a correspondence with learned
men in all parts of the world, and was a contributor to
many ecclesiastical and scientific journals.

Once a year he left Mayfield for his annual visit to
his Alma Mater, St. Sulpice, where my guardian and he
had been fellow-students. The remainder of his time
he spent in the hermit seclusion of study and prayer.
Occasionally we got a glimpse of him on his afternoon
walk—a tall and bent figure, yet lithe and elastic
enough; a gentle, studious face under a broad French
hat, and a profusion of white hair flowing down over
the collar of his coat. We used to salute him, and he
returned the salute as if to perfect strangers—such we
were to him. One alone he recognised—Alfred Coulette,
his protégé. Every Sunday, and on the rather frequent
occasions of some special delinquency, Alfred was ad-
mitted into the sanctuary of the rector's study. Whether
the visit was always agreeable, we could not tell, for
Alfred was very reticent.

The whole control of Mayfield, therefore—tutors,
students, and domestics—was in the hands of Hugh
Bellamy, or "The Grinder," as I shall henceforth call
him. It was his fertile brain that originated, planned,
and conducted the college. He had been a distinguished graduate of Trinity, had taken his degree of
M.A., had been called to the Bar, and made a magnificent début; and with plenty of ambition as a lever,
and cleverness as a pushing force, it was predicted that
he would rise by leaps and bounds in his profession.
Suddenly, and from some cause which we could never
ascertain, he was disbarred, ostracised, beggared. He
hid himself for some years until the memory of this
unpleasantness had subsided, and then commenced life
as a teacher. I have already said that I disliked him;

3

so did Cal, so did Charlie, so did James and Harry
Verdon—two extremely gentle boys, who must have
had a perfect mother. But there was no lack of sympathy between himself and the ill-disposed boys at the
college. They feared him ; but whenever he relaxed,
which was very rarely, he sought them by a kind of
attraction, and felt that there was some invisible tie
between them and himself. A few times he had taken
O'Dell to walk with him. This boy was the ringleader
of mischief in the college, and was almost the incarna-
tion of evil. He was the eldest of four brothers, who
came from Galway—four boys, so untrained, so savage,
so full of impish malice, that to this day I can hardly
believe they were born of Irish parents. They would
have been better classed as the descendants of savage
miners and renegade Indians, such as we meet sometimes in Bret Harte and Cooper. The eldest, Tom, was
the worst ; the second, William, was moulded by him ;
the third, Frank, had some elements of good in his
nature, for he still blushed when detected in crime ;
the fourth was a mere child. But it was these that
planned every wickedness that was perpetrated in the
college. The eldest was, by excellence, the worst. He
had a short, stout frame, exceedingly broad shoulders,
in which his head was sunk without a neck, a heavy,
lumbering gait, a face of deathly pallor, and grey-green
eyes that twinkled in the sunlight. He had supreme,
autocratic control over a dozen boys, whom he inducted
into all manner of wickedness. And he was wicked to
a degree that would be unimaginable if it did not exist
under our eyes. Perfectly passionless himself, and
with every feeling apparently under control, he enjoyed
the conquests of sin and vice in his victims. He
tempted them; and when they fell, he chuckled to
himself with delight, and said, "Good boy!" The
trembling of a young soul under trial, its vain resist-
ings, the delirium when the bounds are passed and sin
is embraced, the bitter remorse that followed, were
delicious to him. He was a past-master in every low

vice. He made young lads smoke; and when they
sickened, he gurgled with suppressed laughter. He
introduced drink, and enjoyed the morning's squeam-
ishness after the night's debauch; and he was backed
up in everything by his second brother, who sometimes
outran him in iniquity. Frank used to interpose occasionally, and cry, "For shame, Tom; the lad will be
sick!" but he was always kicked into silence. It was
Will O'Dell that had blinded Cal's pigeon with a
needle; and this was the cause of the fight in which
Tom O'Dell was defeated by Charlie Travers, and of
which fight there was a commemorative slab rudely
sculptured in the ball-court.

With the exception of Tom O'Dell and another, these
lads were under no special training at Mayfield. They
were sent apparently to be kept out of mischief, not
with any definite designs of receiving an education that
might fit them for life. There were some minor classes
in French and English. At the former, Père Ricard, a
French priest, presided, and had a hard time. At the
latter, the Grinder presided, and the boys had a hard
time. There was one follower of the Evil One who
was under tuition with Cal, Charlie Travers, and myself. His name was Ralph Evans, "rather a respectable
name," Cal used to say, "that might have been borne
by a literary or professional man, who had made his
mark in the world, and might fairly hope for a baronetcy.
How did this Bœotian get it?" For Bœotian he certainly was. He had not a particle of intellect, could not
understand the smallest axiom of science, nor the most
ordinary rules of the Latin Grammar. But he worked
in a manner that would have lifted even an ordinary
intellect into eminence, and he worked entirely by
memory. This faculty he had trained to perfection.
Whole pages of a translation came easy to him; and he
could sing the rules of prosody, and the mnemonic tables
of the grammar, as freely as a ballad. But the moment
a question was asked that demanded the slightest
reasoning, he floundered hopelessly. He was, I am

sorry to say, an object of contempt to two of the tutors—Mr. Dowling, and in a lesser degree to Mr. Ferris, who taught mathematics. Père Ricard pitied him, and Herr Messing's heart was broken by him. Until I understood his character, I thought the tutors rather hard on him. Mr. Dowling spoke of him with the utmost contempt. Mr. Ferris, who was very gentle, used to look quite wearied after the science lesson was over. He preceded me at the science tuition, and came after me to Mr. Dowling; and sometimes the latter used to listen, and call me to listen, to Evans as he waited outside the class hall for me to retire.

"Did you ever hear anything like that before?" Mr. Dowling used to say. "Listen"—

> "Absque, a, ab, abs, and de,
> Coram, clam, cum, ex, and e,
> Tenus, sine, pro, and præ;"

repeated *da capo*. And then half a page of Owgan's translation recited without a mistake.

"Isn't it pitiable? And yet I think I could sympathise with him; but I have heard that he is not the best of a bad set, who are allowed to run a free career of evil in this place. How the fellow has brains enough to be wicked is a puzzle. O'Dell has a certain cleverness about him, although a very ill-visaged fellow indeed. But I suppose Satan supplies this Evans with intellect to know what's wrong, and then loads his memory with evil. I'm told he can recite *Don Juan* through all its disgusting infamy; and that he regularly entertains his own choice circle, not only with stanzas, but even with cantos, of that vile production."

"But isn't it strange that all this is tolerated, and that the respectable boys are in a minority, and the infamous outnumber them?"

"So it is in the world, my friend; and every roof has a world beneath it. And a very rare virtue in those who govern is, an eye clear enough to see what is evil, and a hand firm enough to check it."

Singularly enough, however, the two classes into

which the students were divided rarely came into
collision. There was a kind of mutual understanding
that there should be no open hostilities; although Cal
and the Verdons and Charlie had had a hard time until
the famous victory of the latter. Such petty annoyances
as to be dragged from bed during the night, to find one's
boots full of water in the morning, to be stung by the
bullets of catapults in the study hall, to have ink freely
thrown over one's exercises—all these were of daily
occurrence till Charlie Travers had beaten O'Dell.
That fight was historical. I was told its particulars so
often, that I began to think I had seen it. How
Charlie challenged O'Dell, who accepted with alacrity;
how he felt, during the first round or two, as if he were
beating a bag of sand, and leaving no impression; how
delighted he was when he found O'Dell gasping for
breath, and the beads of sweat shining on his forehead;
and how crestfallen his followers were when O'Dell
shouted " Stop ! " and drew his heavy bulk away. Since
that time the little band were left alone. Insidious
attempts were made to seduce the young Verdons.
They were invited to a supper of cakes and oranges,
and even honey was held out as a bait; and they were
told of the delights of secret drinking, midnight expedi-
tions, etc., to all of which the younger Verdon answered
in a tone of ineffable scorn—

"Where ignorance is bliss,
'Tis folly to be wise."

Yet though there was apparent quiet, there were many
misgivings on the part of the well-disposed lads. They
could not say what a day would bring forth, and there
was the terrible thought that at least one in authority
was in favour of the miscreants. My own coming was
hailed as a good omen; and there was another event in
store for us, which in the beginning looked doubtful
enough, but which afterwards proved of immense service
to us.

This was the advent of a young Frenchman, named

Henri Charcosset, who, to our great surprise, drove up one afternoon in October, and made his début at Mayfield in a high state of anger. He was dressed in superb fashion, *bien chaussé, bien ganté, bien coiffé*, as someone described it; and as such, fell into such immediate contempt with the students at Mayfield, that he was at once nicknamed Monsieur le Comte, or, as an abbreviation, the Count. He spoke English fluently, with just a slight foreign accent, and was quite eloquent in denouncing the brutality and inhospitality of the Irish.

"I did not know I was coming amongst savages," he said; which strong phrase he explained by telling how. when he stepped off the train at Kingsbridge, for he had come *viâ* Bristol and Cork, and remarked that he was a Frenchman, he was immediately assailed with a chorus of sardonic laughter, and such impolite remarks as—

"Yis, another Frinchman from Kerry!"

"Ye're coming to larn ingineering, of course!"

"How did ye lave Marshal Ma~Mahon, sor?"

"And how is Trow-shoe and Canrobert?"

"Thry yer Frinch at him, Jim!"

all of which unintelligible jargon, conveyed in menacing language, and that tone of sarcasm which is quite indigenous to Ireland, set the Celtic temper of the Count on fire with alarm and indignation. He had been hearing and reading of our hospitable and polite people—of the strong ties that bound Ireland to France, etc.—and behold, this is what he saw and experienced! The Grinder, who was obsequiousness itself, endeavoured to soothe him, and get him away from the cool and placid irony of the jarvey, whose face and pantomimic gestures conveyed to us his utter incredulity as to the nationality of the stranger. At last the Count, who was puffing fiercely at a cigar all the time, took up a fistful of silver and flung it contemptuously at the driver, who, paralysed by such a sudden accession of wealth, was stricken dumb, until he was able to gather himself and his reins together, and to say, "Be gobs, perhaps he is a gintleman after all !"

Henri kept sedulously aloof from the body of students for a few days; and we, speculating in boyish fashion about him, concluded he was an effeminate French fop, who would think more of his gloves and ties than of cricket and good conduct. And the first time he appeared amongst us, he glanced over us all with such a supercilious air, and walked off with such contemptuous dignity, that we were quite certain, if he did not prove an enemy, we could hardly expect him to be an ally. We were gravely deceived. Of our own age, he had twenty times our experience; and he was wisely taking notes of us all, before committing himself to any definite decision as to whom he would choose as companions, or enlist as friends. When he did make his choice, we found him a staunch and noble ally, the soul of honour and integrity, quietly and unobtrusively performing little acts of kindness, which he was shy of acknowledging; and he was, moreover, what we were not, a Catholic thoroughly grounded in all the principles of faith, and with a knowledge of the constitution of the Church, its dogmas, its history, and its discipline, which appeared to us as wonderful and unattainable as if we heard he could write Aramaic, or decipher cuneiform inscriptions.

The way in which he rid himself of the advances of O'Dell was characteristic.

The latter, amongst his many accomplishments, affected a great knowledge of horses. It was stylish, and he pretended to style. One day, as the Count was returning from his ride, he walked his horse slowly up the avenue, as the animal appeared slightly lame. He was accosted by O'Dell.

"Dangerous animal to ride any longer, Monsieur !"

"Why ?" queried the Count.

"Dead lame—*laminitis* in the right fore-leg."

Whatever the Count saw in O'Dell's face, he became suspicious and angry, but said nothing. O'Dell, think-

ing he had alarmed him, began to enlarge on the
dangerous and incurable nature of the disorder; and to
show his experience in horseflesh, he stooped down and
laid his hand on the fore-leg of the animal. The Count
touched the horse's flank lightly with his spur, making
him spring forward, and rolling O'Dell over and over on
the gravel; then cantered lightly on to the stable.
O'Dell never discovered what had been done; but he
did not descant again on horses' ailments; and he
never forgave the Count. Thus the latter became a
silent but useful ally of ours.

CHAPTER V

IS THIS FATE?

> " Ernst ist der Anblick der Nothwendigkeit;
>   Nicht ohne Schauder greift des Menschen Hand
>   In des Geschicks geheimnisvolle Urne."
>   SCHILLER.

> " Stern is the onlook of Necessity ;
>   Not without shudder many a human hand
>   Grasps the mysterious urn of Destiny."

WE had rapidly run into October, when the grey frost
shadows linger in the mornings and come back more
early in the cool twilights, and the days are sombre and
sad without the blackness of winter, and the fogs rise
from rivers in the evening, and spread their ghostly
shadows round the shores of seas, and creep into cities,
dimming the gaslights, and bearing with them the first
faint smell of the heavy frosts that are to come. The
beech leaves were reddening in their decay ; and all the
other trees were paling and yellowing, and putting on
their sad consumptive beauty before death. On one of
these soft, grey days, which I have always liked infinitely better than the fierce grandeur of the sun in
July and August, I was walking slowly up and down in

front of the college, trying to remember, by the mere effort of reading it over and over, a certain striking passage in Schiller, which my German tutor, Herr Messing, had shown me that morning. Once, as I turned in my walk, I saw the Grinder leaving the porch, and coming down into the grounds; but I had no idea he was coming to me, until on my return I came quite close to him, and he advanced very cordially, and walked by my side.

"Well, Austin," said he, "and how are you getting on?"

"Pretty well, sir," I said, trying to guess at the same time what in the world he was coming to.

"How do you like your tutors?" he continued.

"Remarkably well," said I, becoming at once enthusiastic; "my Latin tutor appears to me"—

"Yes, yes," said he testily, "I know. Very clever and agreeable and all that; but take care of him, Austin. He has one great fault!"

I listened and waited.

"You'd like to know it?" he continued, turning round and facing me. "Well, it's this. He is an enthusiast, almost a poet, and quite unpractical. Do you know what that man did once?"

I had never heard.

"He sacrificed a position," said the Grinder slowly and deliberately, "worth £800 a year—for what, do you think?"

I said it must have been some great principle.

"Some great principle!" he cried, with a sneer. "No; but for the tense of a Greek verb. As if a Greek verb had nerves and senses to feel, he fought for it against a cross-grained old examiner, and, as usual when people make fools of themselves, he lost."

"But I'll engage, sir," said I, warming up, "I'll engage Mr. Dowling was right, and the examiner was wrong!"

"But, my dear fellow," said the Grinder, "what the mischief is that to any sensible man? Right and

wrong are convertible terms; £800 a year and poverty
are not.   I have some little knowledge of Greek myself;
but I'd let any old fool persuade me that Herodotus
wrote in iambics, and Demosthenes spoke in hexameters,
if it pleased him, and secured a competence for me.
But this is just what I am coming to.   To be practical,
what are you here for?"   He stopped suddenly in his
walk, and faced me.

"I suppose, sir," said I dubiously, "to learn something that would be beneficial to me in after life."

"Precisely," said he.   "But to reduce the question to
its lowest terms, What do you mean by useful?"

"Whatever," said I, hesitating, "that would help to
get me through life."

I knew I was betraying my Master, and talking
awful heresy; but it pleased the Grinder.

"That's just it," said he; "I am glad Dowling has
not utterly spoiled you.   You're here to study just
enough to pass your examination, and you'll have
enough to do.   As to enthusiasm about the Classics,
poetry, etc., that is all —— hosh!   But what do you
think of Ferris?"

Here he bent low, and contracted his already stooped
shoulders, until he appeared only half his size, puckered
his lips, and blinked through his eyes, and said, imitat-
ing to perfection the uncouth accent and manner of my
science tutor—

"Mr. Austin—donche know—I was up last night—
d'ye see—at Grubb's—Grubb's—and I saw Saturn and
his r-rings through the n-new telescope—donche know
—that he is building—d'ye see—for the Vienna Obser-
vatory.   It is grand.   Ah! Mr. Austin, if you'd only
give up these childish classics—donche know—and
study mathematics—do you see?—but don't tell Mr.
Dowling—you'd see—you'd see—Saturn too."

And the Grinder laughed boisterously at this image.

"A fool," said he, "an idiot; but I must tolerate
him."

Now, I was not only surprised at the familiarity of

the Grinder, who rarely noticed me, but I was actually stupefied at the extraordinary likeness between himself and Mr. Ferris, which he put on when mimicking the latter. Ordinarily, no two men could be more unlike. But on this occasion, I could hardly trust my senses, and believe that it was not my poor, quaint, uncouth, and gifted tutor in mathematics. Ugly and ill-favoured he was, stammering and hesitating in teaching, poorly clad and ill fed, but a scholar unquestionably; and my opinion of the Grinder (though I was flattered by his familiarity) did not rise very high, as he ridiculed a man who seemed to me one to be pitied. However, I had not much time for reflection, for my companion just then changed the subject and gave me a fresh surprise. Changing his whole manner and accent, he said slowly and deliberately, eyeing me and measuring me deliberately from head to foot, and then clutching my arm and feeling its muscles—

"I say, Austin, I don't think I should like to get into a tussle with you. You're a well-built fellow. And yet, do you know, I took a prize at wrestling in Trinity a few years ago?"

I was half frightened, and tried to laugh it off.

"I'm sure there is no fear, sir," said I, "that you'll ever have to try my strength."

"I don't know," said he, musing, "I don't know. Strange things happen in this world ; and, say what we like, 'there is a Divinity that shapes our ends, rough hew them how we will'; and there is a something called ἄτη—is it not?—that brings men together, and makes them try conclusions with each other, when they not only do not desire it, but seek to avoid it. The unseen current at the Pole controls mighty argosies on the high seas; and there is some unseen current in our lives that we cannot control or direct, but which masters our fate. However, old fellow," he said, shaking off this melancholy musing, "whatever happens, we won't hurt one another. Shall we?"

I said I hoped not; and stood like a statue gazing at

his tall figure, which went swinging away in his own proud manner across the lawn, and up the limestone steps, and into the darkness of the hall.

Now, I should like to ask metaphysicians or psychologists this question : How did it happen that I, a quiet, easy-going, healthy fellow, whose chief desire was to pass through this world quietly, and give offence to no one, should yet in the short space of one year get into serious conflicts with three persons, one of whom was my most particular friend, and the others, persons I was anxious to avoid rather than seek ?' True, I had a feeling for O'Dell which came very near to hatred, and was quite determined that he should never touch a hair of the head of any friend of mine ; but here was this man, my superior, whom I didn't exactly like, but who had some strange fascination about him on account of his mysterious history, and of all men living I was most anxious to shun him ; yet he has a dim idea that sooner or later we shall get into physical conflict, with the possibility of hurting each other—the very thing most revolting to all my ideas and principles. And we did.

It came about in this manner. However fallen from his high position and degraded in the eyes of men Hugh Bellamy might be, he never lost the hope that sooner or later the Fates would turn in his favour, and enable him to regain the position he had lost, and raise himself even to one more brilliant. To his mind, life was a game of hazard—lose to-day, win to-morrow. Remorse or compunction for evil done never disturbed him. Punishment, as a retribution for guilt, he would not acknowledge. His disgrace was an accident. Thousands of men had done worse and escaped. It was his misfortune to have sinned when the world was in one of its intermittent fits of virtue. He would be more cautious in future, and study the world's wayward temper more carefully. Now, say what we will, there is some subtle fascination for men in such a character, pursuing its course of vice unflinchingly, and with supreme disregard for the world's opinion. There is an attraction about it that excites some admiration in the lower faculties of the soul, though the higher moral sense reprobates and dislikes it. To the end of time, the career of a Napoleon or an Alexander will be spoken of as a career of ruin; and historians will talk of the "demon of destruction stalking through the land, and the pyramids of corpses he has left in his wake"; but they are about the last figures that will perish from the canvas of human history, and to the end they will rivet the attention of men. And so the colossal ambition of Hugh Bellamy had a something in it which we could not help admiring, though now and again the means he employed were revolting even to our untutored moral sense. By some strange fatality I was chosen to thwart him in one of his clever devices to secure the sympathy of some men of "light and leading," whom he had known partially in the brighter days of his life.

An invitation was issued to a large number of men, distinguished in the Church, at the Bar, and in Medicine, to a banquet at Mayfield, to be given on November the First in this year. The invitations were signed by the Father Rector; and an intimation was given that the assembly would be an exceptionally brilliant one, and that a very important consultation would be held on the subject of Catholic education in the country. The college was well known, the rector was universally esteemed as a scholar and as a priest, and scarcely a single apology was received up to All-Hallows Eve.

We, of course, were in high glee. It was to be a gala day for us. The prospect of seeing so many distinguished men, whose names were quite familiar to us, was enhanced by the more carnal anticipations of what Coulette called "a square meal," and others "a good feed." We lent a hand willingly to the decorations of the dining-hall, which was a small, partly detached building erected at quite a late period; and, with its open pitch-pine ceiling and fine windows, it afforded a splendid area for the artistic contrivances of the boys. Young Verdon, with a few bay leaves and laurel, made

a grand scroll of " Welcome " on the main wall over the
principal table ; and, with a ball of twine and a few ever-
greens, we swung festoons from girder to girder of the
roof. The Grinder was in glorious spirits. He laughed
and chatted with us at our work, declared more than
once that we were splendid fellows, and promised us no
end of good things in the future. On the afternoon of
the First, we had a glorious walk all along the seashore,
and returned with furious appetites, which made the
dinner-hour (six o'clock) appear centuries away. We
assembled in the study-hall at half-past five, and
amused ourselves by guessing what kind of old chap
——, Q.C., was, and whether Dr. —— would sing a
comic song. Then Cal mounted a desk, and addressed
us solemnly as follows :—

   " Romans, countrymen, and lovers,

   " ' Hear me for my cause, and be silent that you may
hear.' ' Lend me your ears,' but oh, don't lend me your
appetites ! Dearly-Beloved, we are met on a solemn
occasion ! We are going to be entertained by the élite
of the metropolis. Those great men, whose names are
familiar to you, are going to prove themselves mortals.
They are actually going to eat and drink in your sight.
Do not, I beseech you, allow the strange and unwonted
spectacle to divert your thoughts from the solemn
business before you. If you do not eat and drink, you
shall not become like unto them. Use, therefore, your
time judiciously. Do not waste valuable labour in
pursuing the fleeting attractions of the apple tart, and
the liquid beauties of oscillating jelly. These are an
' unsubstantial pageant—the fabric of a vision.' Lay a
solid foundation of beef and mutton, cement it with
various liquids—that is, if you are allowed a variety—
and then rear, if you like, an ornamental pyramid of
tarts, jellies, and fruits. As master of ceremonies, I
solemnly forbid any quips or cranks to be played until
after the second course has been removed. Any jokes
passed upon bald heads or rubicund noses will be
promptly punished. Evans, I forbid you to put your

knife in your mouth! Your life is a valuable one! If you get lockjaw, think what an orator would be lost to the world! O'Dell, look not on the wine when it is yellow in the glass! You're a heavy fellow, and we should require a door to take you "—

Here O'Dell flung a heavy book with his left hand furiously at the speaker; and I suppose we should have had a scene, but the deep bass of the dinner-gong came ringing through the corridor, and, a few minutes after, we were all seated decorously at table.

The principal table ran across the top of the hall, and the priests and professors and guests sat there—the Father Rector at one end, bowing and smiling, and happy as a child; the Grinder at the other, pale and collected. Mr. Dowling sat almost in the centre, looking, as usual, calm and dignified; and Herr Messing, our German tutor, bland and smiling, sat under the window, facing us. A long table ran at right angles to the first, and here we accommodated ourselves. Everyone was in excellent humour. Waiters in spotless white shirts and swallowtails flitted around the room, and the flowers and glass and piles of fruit gave an aspect of cheerfulness to the place, which we appreciated as a contrast to the dull, gloomy, everyday appearance of the refectory. The soup was passed round, and the conversation began to flow easily from interjections to sentences. Our spirits rose to the occasion, and, in spite of Cal's remonstrances, we indulged in a few feeble jokes on the House of Lords, as we called the upper table. We noticed the absence of Mr Ferris, and were indignant at it; we made signs to Herr Messing, and Cal, putting his hands to his mouth, whispered across the hall, " Ith is grandt"; which gave the professor a fit of choking, and made the Grinder look very cross. The courses were rapidly changed. The wines circulated freely, and all went merry as a marriage bell, when, just as the last dishes were removed, and the dessert plates were being laid, a little shrivelled old fellow, with a face like parchment, who, we understood, was one of the

leading chamber lawyers of Dublin, a litterateur, and a
D.C.L. of Oxford, began to shrug his shoulders, and
complain of the cold. He looked at the windows as
if he felt a draught, and whispered to his neigh-
bour.

The Grinder was at once on the alert.

"Do you feel cold, Mr. Haines? There is no draught,
I assure you; and the day was so close and sultry, I
was afraid the room would be too warm if we had a
fire. Robert, light that stove immediately."

Robert was our general servant—pompous, huge, and
awkward; and to make up for lost time he brought in
a pan of burning coals, which he flung into the stove;
and in a moment the merry blazes were dancing, and
huge volumes of smoke shot through the stove-pipe.
But only for a moment. They appeared to think better
of it; for first one cloud and then another and another
of thick, grimy smoke poured into the dining-room;
and in a short time had filled every crevice and cranny
with their sulphurous fumes, and were wreathing themselves in fantastic clouds against the ceiling.

"Very unpleasant indeed," laughed the Grinder; "it
is the north wind. Singular now that they cannot,
with all the appliances of science, give us a smokeless
stove, or a well-draughted chimney. But it will clear
in a moment when the coals redden."

In came the deadly volumes, however; and now a
cloud of blacks began to descend on dishes and plates,
and old men rubbed their eyes that were pained, and
one or two asthmatic old gentlemen began to cough and
choke with the mephitic fumes.

"It will be all right in a moment," said the Grinder
anxiously. "Robert, remove Mr. Haines' plate, and get
a clean one."

"Would you raise that window a little?" said one of
the asthmatic gentlemen.

"Please, please don't," piped Mr. Haines. "We'll
catch our death of cold."

Herr Messing was blinking and laughing, and then

looking as serious as an owl whenever the Grinder's eyes caught his.

" Better put out the fire," said Mr. Dowling quietly, but peremptorily. The Grinder, who had an extraordinary fear and respect for him, adopted the suggestion.

" Robert, put out that fire, and raise the window." He was very pale and angry. Things were looking so pleasant, and what a little thing should mar them !

" Yesser," said Robert, who returned in a minute with a pail of water, which he flung incontinently into the stove, with the result that a cloud of coal ashes and sulphurous smoke burst forth, and set everyone coughing, whilst we enjoyed the fun immensely.

" Robert," piped Mr. Haines, " would you order my carriage immediately, please ? "

If he had ordered the Grinder to instant execution, the effect could hardly have been more terrible. He grew deadly pale, and we could hear the gnashing of his teeth.

" Don't go," he pleaded, with enforced calmness; "don't go, Mr. Haines ; it will be all right in a moment."

" I think it is better," drawled the querulous old man ; and as he was a great luminary, they all echoed, " It is better," " Quite sorry, I'm sure," etc. ; and in a moment there was a general rising from table, and, coughing, blinking, and complaining, these old Sybarites walked with dignity from the refectory, whilst we tittered, and Cal said in a half-audible voice—

" They might have said grace, at least ! "

The Father Rector and the professors remained at table, whilst the Grinder accompanied his guests to the door. Herr Messing paid most diligent attention to the viands, to our infinite delight ; whilst Father Bellamy declared in his gentlest tones, " It was quite a pity they should go so soon, really. Mr. Dowling, do take a pear. Herr Messing, help yourself to a glass of wine." Which Herr Messing nobly did.

We heard the carriages roll away from the gate, and

4

were conjecturing how the Grinder would look when
he returned. Suddenly I caught the glance of Charlie
Travers fixed on me. He was white and trembling.
He had been trying to attract my attention by coughing
and flinging small pellets of bread across the table,
which I took as play. But the moment he caught my
eye, he leaned across the table, and whispered—

"Goff, we are done for. It is Aunt Sally."

For a moment I did not realise the significance of his
words. When I did, I turned as pale as he, and,
motioning him to remain quiet, I glided from the room.
With my heart beating wildly, I crossed the garden,
and flew upstairs, three steps at a time. Entering
hastily my bedroom, I flung up the window. There,
just a yard away from me, was the top of the stove
pipe, from which a few faint puffs of smoke struggled to
escape. It was six or eight feet down to the leads;
and even had I got on them, it struck me that I was
not tall enough to reach the top of the pipe. In an
agony of fear I ran over every plan in my mind to get
a firm foothold somewhere, and remove the obstruction.
I was helpless. At last I let myself gently down on
the roof of the dining-hall, and, after a few desperate
efforts, in which my hands were cut and burned, I
contrived to displace the top joint of the stove-pipe.
Instantly a fierce rush of smoke shot from the tube;
and I felt that in a few minutes more I should be able
to replace the joint, and escape detection. I sat down
on the leads, and, plunging my hand into the black pipe,
I drew forth the battered and begrimed form of Aunt
Sally, which Charlie and I at the end of September
had stowed away into this receptacle as the handiest
for us, and the easiest to be got at afterwards. I could
not, with all my terror, keep from laughing as I looked
at the stolid painted face before me—the eyes wide
open like a doll's, the nose battered, and the face
blackened and hot from the soot. The joke was a good
one, but serious enough. I lifted the pipe and replaced
it, and it commenced to do its work honestly again;

and, with Aunt Sally in my arms, I lifted myself gently
to the window-sill of my room. I could not have left
it behind, for it would have been a testimony of guilt.
I determined to keep it in some hiding-place for a day
or two, and then destroy it. Fearing to soil my clothes,
I had a good deal of difficulty in climbing, until, near
the top, I flung the detestable thing into the room,
and swung myself in immediately after, *nearly falling
into the arms of the Grinder*. He was standing near the
window, and had watched the whole proceeding, unseen
by me, being concealed in a nook near the wall. He
stood before me now, with his hands behind him, hidden
under his gown, and his eyes burning with excitement
and anger. I thought he would throw me from the
window, but he simply said—

"Take up that thing and follow me."

I took up the wretched image gingerly enough, and
came downstairs. He beckoned me into the study-hall,
and when I had entered he locked the door—a foolish
precaution, for I could have escaped through the window
if I had chosen. I heard his footsteps retreating along
the corridor. Left to myself, I began to conjecture
what he would do. He was in a white rage, and I
thought more of his suppressed anger than if he had
foamed and raved. Then the thought of our conversation a few days previously occurred to me ; and I
began to reflect what I should do, if he offered me
personal violence. I was not afraid of him ; but I had
such pity in my heart for him when I saw how disappointed he was, and reflected that I was the involuntary
cause, that I almost decided to let him have his pleasure
with me, unless he shamed me before the school. The
tread of the boys now echoed along the corridor. The
door opened. The Grinder came in ; and, as the boys
filed into their places, he stood with his hand on the
door-knob. They passed in front of me, all staring at
me and the battered *eikon ;* but I could see Charlie
looking much troubled and depressed, and Cal anxious
and concerned. When they were seated, the Grinder

came over to where I was standing, and, assuming his favourite attitude, he spoke, or rather hissed, as follows:—

"There are certain things which boys do in their recklessness, and they are easily pardoned. There are certain things which deserve the fullest and fiercest condemnation. One of these things has been done this day. Through malice so great that the Archfiend alone could have suggested it, this fellow marred and destroyed a gathering of high and distinguished men—a meeting that might have been pleasant, and certainly would have been profitable. For weeks you looked forward to it. So did I. You looked forward to it with pleasure; I with the desire of gleaning the ideas of distinguished men on an all-important subject, and bringing about conclusions that would be fraught with importance to the entire community. Everything was moving smoothly. Not a single letter of excuse or apology came from men whose time is as precious as gold. Your pleasure and profit have been destroyed, and an insult has been offered to me and to the professors of the college, and the distinguished men who honoured us with their presence, by this miscreant—this ill-con· ditioned, ill-reared, ignorant Tipperary boor, who, through impish malice, put this vile thing," here he kicked it with his foot, " into the stove-pipe, and destroyed the pleasure and harmony of our meeting. It is useless to think now what might have been. It is useless to speculate on the pleasure you would have derived from hearing such men as ——,Q.C., and ——,D.D., turning those periods of eloquence that men go hundreds of miles to hear, or to speculate on the vast consequences that might have arisen from that gathering. That matter is ended. And now, boys, I want an expression of opinion from you about this blackguard act ? "

Charlie stood up, and, with a voice trembling with emotion, said—

" Please, sir, there is some great mistake here. I myself "— when the Grinder cut him short—

" Mistake ? you booby ! Didn't I see the fellow myself, not a quarter of an hour ago, take this thing from the pipe ? Do you take me for a fool ? O'Dell, what say you ?'

" I think, sir," said O'Dell, swaggering, and with an air of conscious virtue, " I think it was a most infamous proceeding."

" You, Evans ? "

The fellow arose, and lisped out—

" Ith wath a mosth dethestable protheeding ! "

" That'll do," said the Grinder, moving to the door. "Now go to your rooms, and leave me to deal with him."

The boys filed out, some looking triumphantly, some commiseratingly, at me. Cal managed to whisper, when passing, " Cry out, Goff, if he hurts you."

The Grinder locked the door carefully, leaving the key in it ; and, with his hands under his gown, strode up and down the room a few times. Then, turning suddenly upon me, he caught me by the lappets of the coat with his two hands, and pushed me back against the wall. I felt his hard knuckles hurting my chest ; and there was a look in his eyes as if he meant murder, and was calculating his chances. Nevertheless, I must candidly say that the uppermost feeling in my heart was one of the deepest pity for him ; for I felt as keenly as if it had happened to myself, his awful disappointment. For a time he eyed me wildly without speaking, still pressing his hands violently against me, and I felt his hot breath fiercely breathed upon me. At length he said—

" Something has been telling me this long time that you, an ignorant lout, are destined to cross me in life. I am sure I don't know why, except that my evil genius has determined to add insult to injury by bringing me into contact with such a fellow. A lion is foiled by a rat ! And certainly you have foiled me with a vengeance, just as my hopes looked bright at last. At this moment I might have been leading and linking to me for ever the men who could command

my future ; and I might have had the proud consciousness that, almost unaided and alone, I had sprung into
position again.   You have foiled me—cleverly, you
lout—successfully, you rustic idiot; but I shall have
my revenge.   I shall not expel you—that would be too
good.   I'll hold you here—here—until "— he pressed
his knuckles more deeply, when suddenly they relaxed.
He lifted his hand hastily to his mouth, whence I had
already seen a tiny red stream trickling—held · his
fingers to the gaslight, became ghastly white, and sank
prostrate and terror-stricken on one of the benches.   It
was really little—so little that it hardly stained the
white handkerchief which, still folded, he took from his
evening dress.   But it must have meant a great deal to
him.   For a time I feared to approach him, for his back
was turned to me.   At last I ventured to say—
    " Can I be of any assistance, sir ? "
He looked at me curiously for a moment, and then
said, rather gently—
    " Leave me, and call Robert ! "
I turned the key gently in the door and went out.
The boys were hidden away behind pillars and in the
projections of the arches, and I was assailed with
questions: " What happened, Austin ? "   " Did he hurt
you," etc., etc. ; and one, more venturesome than the
rest, peeped through the keyhole, and, seeing the Grinder
prostrate on the form, came to the conclusion: " By
Jove ! Austin has licked him."   I told one of the
young lads to fetch Robert; and, going upstairs to my
room, sick and disgusted, I flung myself on my bed.   I
felt as if I had been guilty of a great crime ; and
though my conscience whispered, " You have done
nothing consciously wrong," still I could not help
feeling that I was the unconscious instrument of evil to
one I was anxious rather to serve.   And so I lay still,
and fretted and worried myself, until near nine o'clock,
when the familiar scratching at the door meant
Charlie; and he came in, bringing a cup of tea, and
saying, the dear fellow—

" I knew you wouldn't like to come down."   Yet he refrained, like a true gentleman, from asking a single question.

But I told him all.   And we reasoned the matter out together very calmly—

> "The sad, mechanic exercise,
> Like dull narcotics, numbing pain."

CHAPTER VI

HERR MESSING

"Das Herz und nicht die Meinung ehrt den Mann."
                                        SCHILLER.

"Our own heart, and not other men's opinions, forms our true honour."—COLERIDGE's Translation.

THE feeling that you have been the unwilling cause of trouble to others is more intensely painful than the consciousness of guilt.   For it is more flattering to our vanity to know that we suffer the consequences of our own acts, than to feel that we are but blind instruments in the hands of Fate.   And whatever retribution comes to us appears to be adequate to our guilt; whereas the punishment and remorse of unconscious ill-doing are altogether beyond what we have deserved.   For several days after the events narrated in the last chapter, I was the most miserable of mortals.   I had indeliberately inflicted two deadly blows on a man to whom I owed, and certainly felt, no malice.   I had blasted his life-prospects, and probably imperilled his life itself.   And what made the position most odious to me, was the reflection that the school looked up to me as a hero; and I got no blame, but a great deal of praise, for my pluck in doing what I would have considered a most dastardly act if it had been deliberate.   And when boys came up to me and said, "Austin, you have taught the Grinder a lesson for life," I only thought,

with feelings which are indescribable, of that tiny red
stream which I saw flowing from his mouth, and his
sad exclamation: "Ah! mother!"   Occasionally, a
word would be said that would bring a momentary
consolation, as when Mr. Dowling exclaimed: "Now,
look here, Austin; this is all nonsense. You have done
a good turn to society and the world by checking that
fellow's ambition.   If you knew all, you would fret
less!"   Then I begged and prayed him to tell me all.
But no! it was a secret, and he would not divulge it.

Mr. Ferris was in real anguish about the unfortunate
affair.   He questioned me in his own timid way about
the whole event; but when I mentioned by chance how
indignant we all were when we found him excluded
from the dinner, he only lifted his hands and said,
"Don't—don't mention it!   Poor Hugh! Poor Hugh!"
From which I concluded that he must have known the
Grinder in early life, and probably had been at the same
school.   Yet, a few days after, he, generally so gentle,
got into a furious passion with Evans, and actually beat
him with all the severity of a quiet man, when the
fellow hinted that I had acted maliciously throughout:
an event which appeared insignificant, but was fraught
with sad consequences for poor Ferris.

Charlie was, as usual, very grave about the whole
affair.   Cal laughed at it, and reminded me of Coulette.
Henri said, in his easy, off-hand manner, "Soyez
tranquille, mon ami! cela n' a pas arrivé sans dessein";
and when I looked indignant at this, he quietly added,
"a part des dieux."   He ordered his horse, and rode
out for the evening.

My principal consolation came, however, from a
source to which I owe more than half the education I
received at Mayfield, and all the strength which has
sustained me since then.   I have mentioned the name
of Herr Messing incidentally here and there in this
narrative, and, perhaps the reader would judge, with
but small respect.   Yet I never write that name but
with the wish that my pen was of gold, and my letters

gilded and indelible. Child and philosopher, uncouth
and sublime, passing from the accidents of life, which
affected him deeply, to its more solemn mysteries and
meanings, where he found his hope and rest, he was the
most attractive character that has come across my
vision in life. Like all other characters worth studying,
it was a long time before I got inside the shell which
everyone must wear nowadays, as a protection from an
irreverent and scoffing world. I attended his class in
German, smiled at his bad English, laughed at his bad
temper, and thought no more about him. But as I
seemed to be more interested in "my Schillare" and
"my Goethe," as he called his poets, than the ordinary
run of our students, who detested German, partly on
political, principally on philological principles, we grew
into one another's sympathies, and he gave me credit
for a love of German which I was far indeed from
possessing. "That barbarous jargon," Mr. Dowling used
to call it; "that simian chatter," Monsieur le Comte;
and my own opinion nearly coincided with theirs: but
it was part of our programme.

One day, however, I heard a violent commotion in
Herr Messing's room, which was just opposite mine on
the same corridor. He had rushed up the stairs,
slammed the door behind him, and I could hear him
striding up and down his room, declaiming in most
unintelligible language against someone that had
angered him. I thought it my duty to go over and
see him; and I found him in a violent fury.

"Dot idiot—dot vhool—dot dummlopf! Gott im
Himmel! what hof I done? Did I murder? No!
Did I steal? No! Why has Himmel punished me by
zending me to dis blace? Do you know what dot
vhool did ask me? Did Schillare write in French?
My Schillare! my tevine Schillare! dot zang in his
Zherman tongue his tevine inspirations! What do I
do here? I vhill go! I vhill not ztay!"

"Look here, mein Herr," said I; "what is it all
about? Who abused Schiller?"

"Dot vhool! dot Evans!"

"Oh, is that all?" said I, laughing. "Evans will bo tried for manslaughter one of these days. He is slowly killing Mr. Dowling; and Mr. Ferris, I know, is going down into a premature grave. And now he has attacked you with his stupidity. It is the old story of the lion that died of an ass's kick. But really, Herr Messing, how can you be angry with that fool?"

"You are right," said the professor gleefully, "you are right. You are mein vrendt!"

"And now, professor," said I, "let me hear that famous Sword-song you are always talking about."

"I don't zing, I don't zing, mein vrendt," said the professor; "but I will recite it."

"No, no, Herr Messing," said I; "you must sing it as you sang it, with a pot of lager beer before you, in Heidelberg. Out with it!"

Delighted beyond measure, the professor deliberately threw off his coat, turned up his shirt sleeves, opened his trunk, and, taking out twc pretty rusty swords, handed me one. I ran my finger along the edge. It was blunted and notched.

"Mein vrendt," said the professor, "it has zeen zervice. But lift it up now, and you zay nothing. To-morrow you shall zing it with me."

So I heard for the first time the brave Sword-song of Körner, and a grand dithyramb it is. And we clashed the weapons together at "Hurrah!" and became the fastest friends from that hour.

And now in my boyish sorrow he found me out, and in his own uncouth way tried to solace me.

"Now, why do you vret? He is not det. He still live. He did not eat a goot dinner dot evening. Dot is true. But whose fault is dot?"

"Ah, but, Herr Messing, it was horrible to see that blood flowing."

"Yes! but did you make dot plood? Where did it goom vrom?"

"From his lungs, I'm sure. That's the worst of it It means fatal disease and death."

"Oh, I zee you've studied medicine. I vhill goom to consult you in future. But did you give him dot disease? Did his gonsumption goom vrom you?"

"And then," I continued, following my own thoughts, "that cry about his mother! I'll never forget it, professor—never!"

"But, mein Gott!" he cried, getting excited, "did you kill his mother?"

I could not help laughing at the quaint logic of my friend, a fact which his kindness instantly seized upon.

"Ah, now you laf! Dot is good! Goom! put on your coat, and we vhill vhalk."

He used to call me the Azdronomer-Rol (Astronomer-Royal). For, one evening, Mr. Ferris persuaded me to go with him to Grubb's, and see the lenses for the new telescope to be built at Vienna. I induced the professor to come also. And on a cold, frosty night, when the stars were blazing, and there was no moon up to obscure their splendours, we took our places at the end of a queue in the grounds where Mr. Grubb was fashioning this beautiful telescope. And for hours we shivered and trembled; and the professor declared he would go home, and Mr. Ferris begged us to remain · and at three o'clock in the morning, when Orion was flashing away in the south, we got a peep at Saturn, and very wonderful it was, and at the nebula of Orion, which was yet more wonderful. But the professor, who tried to look with his two eyes wide open through the object-glass, declared he could only see "de dark"; and he said that it was all "dom humbug"; and he dubbed Mr. Ferris "dot impostor," and myself "de Azdronomer-Rol."

"Goom now, my Azdronomer-Rol," he said, this gloomy day, "and we vhill go down to Zandycove, and zpend the day there. And we vhill read Schillare together. Mein vrendt," he said sententiously, as we moved briskly along the road, that was slushy in the thaw, and thick with blackened leaves—"mein vrendt, we have enough to do in repenting of our sins, without vretting about our mistakes."

And on the rocks at Sandycove we sat then and many a day, watching with delight the breakers surging up, and groping like the hands of the blind along the channels of the rocks, and falling away, broken into sheeted foam, and, unconscious of defeat, leaping up again, and sweeping in glistening lines along the adamant, and hissing and struggling and hoarse with many murmurs, and redolent of the salt odours of purity and incorruption.

CHAPTER VII

THE FATHER RECTOR

'My dear friend and teacher Lowell—right as he is in almost everything—is for once wrong in these lines—

'Disappointment's dry and bitter root,
Envy's harsh berries, and the choking pool
Of the world's scorn, are the right mother-milk
To the tough hearts that pioneer their kind.'

They are not so; love and trust are the only mother-milk of any man's soul. So far as he is hated and mistrusted, his powers are destroyed."
RUSKIN's *Modern Painters.*

I WAS beginning to recover my equanimity, especially as the Grinder was now apparently recovered and going about his duties as usual, and the event was half forgotten, when one day, after a walk with the professor, I was summoned to the Father Rector's room. This was unusual enough to be ominous for me; and it was with a considerable amount of fear I entered the Father Rector's presence. The room was warm, and the whole atmosphere was filled with the smell of books. No wonder. They lined the walls from floor to ceiling, and appeared to be pushing one another, as if trying to escape from the pressure. The floor was littered with them, and the tables were laden and overflowing with them—books of all shapes and sizes and bindings, that would have made the heart of a student leap with joy. Rusty old folios, barred and blackened by centuries of hard work in foreign monasteries, with just here and there a speck of gilding remaining to remind us of their ancient splendour— stately quartos in somewhat better condition, but dirty and grimy—smiling octavos in all the glory of new binding, and flashing with gold letters on crimson or blue morocco—and coquettish little duodecimos that seem made up to be kept in the pocket, and produced on the lonely walk or the quiet rest by the seashore. And on the centre table, grim and black, with here and there a flash of brass or nickel, were batteries and retorts; for the rector was a scientist as well as a litterateur. He was seated near one of these as I entered, and motioned me rather kindly to a chair near him.

"I have sent for you, Mr. Austin," said he calmly, but with the preoccupation of a student, "about some letters I received yesterday, and the purport of which I did not understand until I had consulted Mr. Bellamy. I must do Hugh the justice to say that he did not mention this unpleasant business to me until I had spoken to him. Yet he has suffered. Poor fellow! You know his mother was very delicate. Indeed, I warned my poor brother not to marry her, for I could see clearly she had a tendency to phthisis; and I fear Hugh—that is, Mr. Bellamy—has inherited it. Pity— he is so good and so clever. Now, I never suspected there was anything wrong about that dinner. I thought things were going on very well. Didn't you?"

Seeing me somewhat embarrassed, he recollected himself.

"Oh! I beg pardon, Mr. Austin. But what are you studying?"

I told him.

"Well, now," the old man continued, soliloquising,
"I used be very fond of Greek myself; but you see I
am getting old, and really Greek pains my eyes; and
though I like to read it, I have been obliged to give it
up.   But you are learning physics—are you not?"

I told him I was merely getting through the pre-
paratory stages.

"Ah, well," he said, "it will all come in time.   But
now," he said, rising up and going over to one of his
batteries, "look at this!   Isn't it pretty?"

I bent over the cells, and the villainous acids made
me cough and sneeze.   But the rector, unheeding,
went on as if he had a class before him, explaining the
nature of electricity, and currents, and positive and
negative poles, until I, who had insensibly imbibed Mr.
Dowling's distaste for science, began to think that I
would have preferred the expected scolding.   After an
interval, however, he said kindly—

"I see you're tired.   But what message have you
brought me?   My memory is failing, too, I fear," he
added, in a melancholy tone.

"It was about some letters, sir," I said, "which you
had received."

"Ah, yes, I remember," he replied.   "There was one
letter to me from your guardian, and one for yourself.
Here it is.   You can read it at your leisure.   But now,
like a good boy, don't play any more practical jokes.
I know there is not much harm in them," he continued,
as he saw me about to explain; "boys will be boys.
But you remember that story of Voltaire and the old
Jesuit; and how he was disrespectful towards the Holy
Name, and the old father prophesied an evil future for
him.   And, indeed, I remember a young fellow who
studied with your guardian and myself at St. Sulpice—
a clever young fellow, brilliant, with a marvellous taste
for the languages—he spoke Latin nearly as well as
Père Gosselin himself—well, he hasn't come to much.
Poor Ernest! I used say to him, 'Keep to the Catechism,
Ernest; hold fast to your beads!'   He always laughed.

And now—Rénan! a name that is detested by the
Christian world! But you won't turn out badly, will
you?" the old man said affectionately, rising up and
placing his hand on my head. I knelt instinctively for
his blessing; and he said, " Come and see me sometimes,"
and dismissed me.

I think it was well that the old priest's blessing
descended upon me, for I suppose I should have sinned
deeply when, opening the letters, I discovered an
infamous plot to wound me in the keenest manner, by
persuading my poor guardian to believe that I had
rapidly become —— well, what I was not. The Father
Rector had placed two letters in my hands—the one
addressed to the Rev. T. Costelloe, P.P.; the other,
my guardian's remonstrance to myself. The first was
anonymous, and, written in a boy's hand, ran thus :—

" REVEREND FATHER,—1 think it is a duty I owe to
you to inform you that Geoffrey Austin, your ward, is
going on badly here. I know it is not exactly my
province to communicate this to you; but Father
Bellamy and his nephew are so kind that they do not
like to pain you, and they have some hopes that he will
yet amend. He has mixed himself up with a bad set
in this house; and is a great friend with some of the
tutors, who, living outside the college, *know too much.*
He has been detected lately as the principal in a shameful conspiracy to injure Mr. Bellamy, by making him
ridiculous before a very distinguished company of
learned men who were dining here; and the result of
this was, that Mr. Bellamy got hæmorrhage from the
lungs, and his life is still in danger. If you think that
you ought not credit this letter, as anonymous, write
yourself to the Father Rector.—Recommending myself
to your pious prayers, I remain, Rev. Father,

" ALUMNUS."

The letter from my guardian to myself was as
follows :—

" My dear Geoffrey,—It was with feelings of unspeakable sorrow that I read the enclosed letter, and the sad confirmation of the truth contained in it, which I received subsequently from Mr. Bellamy. I know well, alas! the sad temptations which beset young souls when, on entering life, they are cast into the society of men whose knowledge is beyond their wisdom; and who, having tasted the bitter fruit, are anxious to make clear to others also the difference between good and evil. But, my dear boy, I have received a severe shock to find that so soon you should have forgotten the high principles of your youth, and, above all, indulged in that reckless disregard for the feelings and happiness of others, which I always considered the vice most foreign to your character. When I remember the last words we had together only a few months ago, and your remarks on certain professions, I find it still very hard to believe that the whole sad business is not a mistake, and that a boyish freak may not have been interpreted as an act of more than boyish malice. But I have before me the testimony of the man who was most aggrieved; and he writes, let me say, in sorrow more than in anger, and 'regrets more deeply the perversion of your moral principles than the accident that has occurred to himself.' These are his words. I can now only conjure you, by the memory of all you hold dear, and by your last promise to me on your mother's grave, to pause in time, and retrace the steps you have taken. The future is still yours—to make or to mar, for better, for worse; and I shall be the first to forget this breach in our happy relations, when I am assured that you regret the cause, and have become again your old self.—I am, my dear Geoffrey, yours affectionately in Christ,   T. Costelloe."

I read that letter, line by line, twice, walking up and down in the ball-court to the rear of the college; and now, after the lapse of eight years, when I take it out, dog-eared and frayed and yellow, from my desk, I think I see every letter of it, feathered with flame, as I saw it on that day. Certainly the Grinder had taken an exquisite revenge. If he had beaten me to the point of death, and expelled me, I would have felt it less keenly. But to disgrace me in the eyes of the man whom I loved best in all the world, and this without hope of explanation—for my pride would not permit me to explain—this was the perfection of hatred. I do not know how the time flew by, as I paced up and down the concrete floor of that ball-court. Then I determined to show no sign to the Grinder or his allies that I had suffered; but man needs some help, so I sought out Charlie. He was studying very hard of late, and I found him deep over his books; but the dear fellow saw at once that I was in trouble, and did all he could to relieve me. We talked the matter over and over, and then Charlie went out to look for Cal. Delighted to get an excuse to escape for a chat, Cal came in, in glorious spirits, flung himself down on Charlie's bed, and scrutinised both letters in true detective style.

"Of course you'll write to Father Costelloe," said Charlie to me.

"No," said I, "certainly not. When he has chosen to judge me without a hearing, I am not going to make a defence."

"I think you ought."

"That's quite out of the question," I said.

"One little word will make all right."

"Not at all, my dear fellow. Piles of foolscap will not clear me now. I must leave it to time."

"'Ἰού, ἰού, ἐκότου," cried Cal, who was just then studying Œdipus, and was racking his brains to get at the author of the letter. "I've seen it somewhere," he said, knitting his brow; "but where, where? Stop a moment," he cried, rushing from the room. In a few minutes he returned with a notebook, containing the signature of every professor and pupil in the house—however he obtained them—pasted in clearly and carefully.   After a long and most diligent investigation, he exclaimed, " Eureka !   I thought I knew it . That sneak and scoundrel Evans!   Look at this! ' Yours sincerely,' letter for letter ! "

" Cal, my boy," said Charlie, " you'll do credit to the force yet.   Lecocq was nothing to you.   It is quite clear the Grinder employed that little wretch to write the letter; and he had not brains enough to make a decent disguise of his handwriting."

" What will be done now ? " said Cal.

" What can be done ? " said I.

" I'd write if I were you," said Charlie again, persuasively.

" Impossible, Charlie," said I.   " Let us dismiss the matter."

That evening I wrote a curt acknowledgment of the receipt of five pounds to Father Costelloe; and not a word on the main subject of the letter.   And so a breach was made that widened into a gulf, which was not bridged for many years.   Our correspondence thenceforth, after a few letters from my guardian, pleading and piteous enough, but to which I was too proud to respond, was limited to the forwarding and acknowledgment of the occasional cheques that went to meet my requirements.

CHAPTER VIII

MR. FERRIS DISMISSED

"Mine enemy builded well, with the soft blue hills in sight,
    But betwixt his house and the hills, I builded a house for spite ;
And the name thereof I set in stone-work over the gate,
    With a carving of bats and apes : and I called it the House of
    Hate."

IT was just a few days before the Christmas holidays that Mr. Ferris announced to us that he was severing his connection with the college. Just after his hour's lesson, he said in his shuffling way to Charlie—

"Good-bye, Mr. Travers, good-bye!"

"Good-bye," said Charlie dubiously; and then looked questioningly at his tutor.

"But, donche know? I'm not coming back any more," said Mr. Ferris.

"Wha-a-t?" cried Charlie; "you don't mean to say you're going to leave Mayfield?"

"Indeed'n I am," said Mr. Ferris. "You're getting a new tutor, a great deal cleverer than I, donche know? But I think I did my work honestly, donche know?" said the poor fellow, almost in tears.

"But what in the name of Heaven are you going for?" said Charlie; "are you going of your own accord, or are you dismissed?"

"Dismissed," said the tutor sententiously. "Hugh— that is, Mr. Bellamy—donche know—has told me that my services won't be required after Christmas."

"But what reason did he give? What have you done? I'm sure your pupils are satisfied with you."

"Ah, well, it makes no matter. There's a mystery, donche know?"

"Cal and Austin will be awfully cut up, I know," said Charlie. "But is there no chance of keeping you? Suppose we drew up a requisition, or a round-robin, or something"—

The tutor shook his head mournfully, and went away. Now, we were awfully disturbed at this, for somehow we had grown very fond of the quaint, poor teacher; and then it was pretty clear that he was not well circumstanced in life, and, if dismissed, would have to face poverty. But the mystery of his dismissal —what was it? He had licked Evans well. Evans was a pet of the Grinder's. Could that be it?

"No," said Monsieur le Comte, "that's not it!"

"Then you know, Henri—you know something?" said Charlie.

"Just a little," said Henri, with the air of one who

knew a great deal, but would be very sparing of his information.

"Tell us, Frenchy; tell us," cried Cal, to whom a secret held by another was a torture.

The Count looked over Cal superciliously, drew the eternal cigarette from his lips, sent a puff of blue smoke into the air, and was silent. He was insulted.

"I say, Henri," said Charlie diplomatically, "don't mind Cal. But I'll tell you what you'll do. Tell us the whole thing in French. French is the language of history, and all important events should be told in that sublime language. Besides, it will be an exercise for us."

Henri took the bait, and commenced—

"I ride out sometimes, as you know"—

"Parfaitement," interjected Cal. "I mean," continued he, as he saw the Count again offended, "that we have often admired your horsemanship." This was too much for Coulette, who had heard Cal a score of times ridiculing the Frenchman for the awkward manner in which he rode. So he ran; and for the next hour went pacing up and down a path he had worn for himself under the limes, chuckling and laughing to himself the while.

"Well," continued the Count, "on one occasion I saw that *cochon* Evans prowling round the streets, and I rode after him at a distance, keeping my eye upon him. He used watch poor Ferris leave Mayfield, and take the tram into the city; and several evenings Evans took the inside seat of the tram, whilst Ferris was perched outside. The latter used get off when he came in near Baggot Street, and look around anxiously, with his heavy books under his arm; then would rush down a by-lane and disappear. A few times, Evans, after a short interval, followed him down the lane; and I used ride by, and, doubling back quickly, would find the fellow at the corner, generally engaged in staring at the pavement and chewing tobacco. The fellow always looked so puzzled that I think he cannot have found anything except the address at which Ferris lived."

" Is that all ? " cried we in chorus.

"C'est tout ! " said the Count blandly, and walked away smoking.

It was unsatisfactory enough, but it gave us a clue of an important nature, which we were determined to follow up. Evans was at the bottom of the whole plot; and he had evidently made a report of such a nature that the Grinder had thought fit to dismiss Mr. Ferris on the strength of it. Now, the question was, What report had Evans furnished? Was there any foundation for it? We talked over the matter repeatedly— Charlie, Cal, and I, for M. le Comte troubled his mind no further on the matter; and Coulette was too absorbed in his own desires to be free from the " infernal place," that he cared little about the troubles of anyone else. The other boys rarely referred to it; except that that one day O'Dell told Cal, as if it were a great discovery, that old Stutterer was going, and a tremendous fellow coming over from Oxford in his place. During those days, too, the Grinder used to eye us suspiciously, as if there were a movement on foot to counteract him. He never spoke to me; but he did say to Charlie, " You are getting a new tutor, Charles, in science. We must brush up there; I am afraid we have lost time already." And he ventured much the same information in French to Monsieur le Comte, who merely lifted his eyebrows and said " Pardon ! " and the Grinder did not continue the conversation.

Now, the thought that there was some direct relationship between the Grinder and poor Ferris was haunting me these days. I remembered the appearance of the former the famous evening in October; and then there was the familiarity, so promptly checked, when Ferris, speaking of the Grinder, would, when off his guard, call him Hugh. Either they were schoolfellows, or else, relations. But surely not the latter! What relationship could there be between uncouth Mr. Ferris

and the superb Hugh Bellamy, who cut his most
ordinary sentences by rule, and appeared, by his
precision and pomp, to be always addressing in imagination " My Lord." And then, surely, if there were any
family ties between them, would not the Father Rector
be equally related to them both ? and would he not
recognise in some way the needy tutor ? Yet he never
spoke to him, or noticed him ! There was a mystery.
Who would solve it ?

We tried many plans, but failed utterly. We
followed the trail of poor Ferris, and actually saw Evans
dogging his footsteps ; but we were always restrained
from pushing our inquiries too far, lest we should
wound the susceptibilities of the poor tutor. At last
matters came to an issue, for we learned that, on the
last schoolday before the Christmas holidays commenced,
Mr. Ferris was to be paid off and dismissed.

It was four o'clock on a dark winter's evening ; the
classes were over, and Cal reported that Mr. Ferris had
remained behind in the classroom, instead of going
home as usual.

"Now, we'll slip out through the refectory window,"
said Cal, " creep along near the classroom window to
the front where a pane of glass is broken—accidentally,
of course—and I have drawn the big black-board in
front, so that we can hear, if there be anything worth
hearing, without being seen."

We made some objection to this plan as not being
quite honourable ; but what is honour before the
sublime passion of curiosity ? We did as Cal directed,
and we were in our appointed places at a few minutes
after four.

Mr. Ferris was in the classroom, sitting on one of the
forms, and leaning heavily on the desk near him. His
head was resting on his hands. We could not see his
face. In a few minutes the Grinder came in, walked up
in his usual swinging way, and, folding his arms, looked
down on the poor tutor.

" So," said he at last, with a peculiar sting of sarcasm

in his voice, "this is my return for all that I have done
for you? This is your gratitude for all my kindness?"

"I don't understand you, Hugh," said the poor tutor,
without looking up; "what have I done to offend you?"

"Done!" cried the Grinder; "you have done the
very last thing an amorphous creature like you should
have done. Weren't you miserable enough without a
slattern to share your misery? But possibly, for
human folly is infinite, you thought yourself an Adonis,
and fascinated this wretched girl, whom I presume you
have married. Now, sir, this is a celibate establishment;
we want no uxorious pedagogues here. I took you from
the gutter, and made you a gentleman. You have made
a choice without consulting me. Go, and be happy
with your Aspasia!"

"Who told you this?" said the tutor, in gentle
surprise.

"No matter who told me," said the Grinder angrily;
"you are living with a woman, who, I presume, is your
wife, for I understand she welcomes you home in wifely
fashion. What exquisite taste that woman has!"

"She is not my wife," said the tutor meekly.

"What!" said the other, more exasperated than ever;
"do you tell me she is not your lawful wife? By H——s!
I am beginning to respect you. So you are a fast man,
by Jove! You, the saint, the hermit, the recluse,
actually indulging in this mighty luxury! What next?
Ortolans and champagne—down to Killiney by moonlight—and guinea tickets to the Opera with Lais! Give
me your hand, what I never asked you for before, you
delicious reprobate'—

"Stop, Hugh," said poor Ferris, just a little sternly;
"this is ribald language. She is Elsie—your sister!"

If the worst insult that ever fell from human lips
had struck him, the Grinder could not be more enraged
than at these simple words. His face, always white,
became more ashen than ever, and the features appeared
to be drawn down from the eyes and about the lips
as on the faces of the dead.

"And, you hound," he cried, "you dare tell me this! You dare tell me that I have been supporting, through the salary I flung to you in compassion, that curse and bane of my life—that girl! Surely this is the worst evil that has ever befallen me!"

"Elsie is your sister," said the tutor meekly.

"No, no, not my sister," said the Grinder. "I have cut her image and her picture from my heart long ago. It was in her degradation I was dragged down."

"No, no," said the tutor meekly; "you sinned yourself."

"Did I?" cried he. "Yes; but I might have sinned a thousand times, and the world would have honoured me for it. But her disgrace fell upon me, and bespattered me, and made me, God, what I am — a schoolmaster!"

He walked up and down the room, greatly agitated, for some minutes, and then turned sharply to his brother.

"Look here, Alf," said he; "old fellow, I don't want to beggar you. Keep on as you are—on one condition!"

"What is that?" said the tutor.

"Dismiss that girl," cried the Grinder. "Remove the pollution of her presence—let her go back to the slums whence you have taken her; let her have the fate she has selected; let her sleep in the flare of the gas-lamps, and hide her face from the sun—and I will stand by you for ever!"

"The proposal is a shameful one," said the tutor. "Give me what you owe me, and let me go."

"Go, then," said his brother; "but remember, that never, never am I to see your or her face again. I have certain things to do in life. I am not to be balked by fools and night-birds."

"May God forgive you!" said the tutor meekly. "Elsie and I will pray for you."

The Grinder looked him all over in scorn, and proceeded to count his salary, and write his receipt.

"Heaven is always with the biggest battalions. Now go."

The tutor put out his hand, but the Grinder put it away rudely, and stalked from the room. Then Mr. Ferris took out a very poor, stained red handkerchief, and wiped his eyes, and folded his money, in a knot, in the corner of the handkerchief. Then he took up his hat, and looked around. There was something, I suppose, even in the ink-bespattered, well-sculptured desks that affected him deeply, for he continued gazing at them for a long time. Then he passed over to the walls where the old familiar diagrams were hanging, and in the dim December twilight he peered at them, and passed his fingers over them lovingly. And, taking up a piece of chalk, he came to the black-board, behind which we were hiding, and we could hear his fingers nimbly passing over the board in pursuit of some favourite problem. He paused, and, heaving a sigh, he whispered, *"Quod erat demonstrandum,"* and went away. Words which will be repeated by many human lips until the great Geometer comes at the last, and solves all the problems that distract humanity, and wipes out the foolish diagrams of men by the great irrevocable decision ! But as the poor tutor passed down under the limes, with bent head and wavering footsteps, three figures sprang on him from the night shade of the dark trees, and wrung his hands till he cried out, and bade him cheer up and be trustful.

And on Christmas Eve, the same three, with another, who would not take the cigarette from his mouth, even when scaling the walls, took a heavy hamper from the tram that stops at a certain corner of Baggot Street, and pulled it along a lonely lane, till they stopped before certain railings, and gently pulled a shabby doorbell. A young girl came to the door—fair, but with a sad look—and, in answer to her almost frightened inquiries, she was bidden tell the tutor that a " foreign gentleman " wanted him on business. But the others intervened, and said—

" Tell Mr. Ferris that some old friends have called

to see him, but he is not to come down for ten minutes."

So they went into the hall, and into the dingy parlour, where there was a strong smell of cigars (the tutor's only weakness), and they opened the hamper, and heaped its miscellaneous contents on the table, having previously pushed away the shabby astronomies, slates, and papers with dismal hieroglyphics; and then they sat down and waited, and looked around at the prints on the wall, and the paper flowers on the mantelpiece, and studied, with many a profane exclamation, the faded photograph of a young gentleman in white nankeen, who was just engaged in the act of lifting his bat and sending a ball into utmost space, and in whom they recognised the Grinder.

But there was a shuffling of feet upon the stairs, and a whispered consultation in the hall, and the door opened, and the tutor came in, blinded and dazed. We gave him three tremendous cheers, and Hip! hip! hurrah! and wished him a Merry Christmas, and slapped him on the back till he gasped for breath, and could only say—

"Mr. Austin, I wish you—How are you, Mr. Cal ?"— which made Cal roar, and the tutor confused; and then we sat down as calmly as we could, and told him there were a few Christmas presents that we thought he would like, we got them from home, etc., etc.

"Oh, but, douche know ? they are so valuable," said the tutor, quite overwhelmed.

"Not at all; they cost nothing," said Cal. "Just taste that bit of cake, old fellow; and, look here, have you any glasses here ? "

He couldn't say, but Elsie knew. So Elsie came in; and we saw the very beautiful girl who had opened the door for us, but a great deal more like the Grinder than the tutor. And she was very proud, too, and looked quite grand, and put down the glasses with the air of a princess. But she thawed when she knew we were her brother's friends; and we made the poor man swallow two glasses of port in rapid succession, which scalded him and made him cough, and we talked and chatted and laughed till the clock struck ten. We rose to go.

"Well, old fellow," said the privileged Cal, "the Catechism says the good must suffer, and the wicked prosper. But, thank God, there is a Hell hereafter."

"Don't say that, don't say that!" said the tutor in alarm; "we must all forgive."

"Forgive!" said Cal indignantly; "there is altogether too much forgiveness in this world. The Christian religion ought not to be preached or practised to savages like the Grinder."

"Oh, hush! hush!" said the tutor.

"It is an infernal shame," said the Count, "that you should be turned away. There's no justice at all in this world!"

And so in different ways we expressed our angry affection for the poor tutor, the sister all the time smiling at our impetuosity; for I notice that women seldom trouble themselves about abstract principles of right or wrong, when their feelings or affections are preoccupied.

But at last the tutor took down from the mantel-piece an illuminated scroll, which in red and gold told the angel's message on that night when Truth and Justice met, and Mercy and Peace did kiss. He held it up for us to read, shading with his fingers the words, "To men of good will."

"Yes," said Charlie; "but you are mutilating, or rather improving on, the text. Take away your hand, and let us read the whole."

But the tutor put the scroll gently away, and said—

"I have improved the angel's message. But so, too, did Emmanuel!"

CHAPTER IX

A PHILOSOPHICAL CHAPTER.

" In the still hour, when passion is at rest,
Gather up stores of wisdom in thy breast,
So when the storms awake, and in the din
Imprudence or malevolence to sin
Should tempt thy frailty, thoughts of wisdom stored
Shall check the passion ere its tides are poured."

SPEAKING of those things to my mentor, Herr Messing,
who, although he had no relish for science, had always
a kind word and generous sympathy for the weak, I was
rather surprised at the bitter and cynical way in which
he spoke. He seemed to be as little surprised at the
cruelty and injustice of men, as if he had only witnessed
the swoop of a robin on a worm, or a hawk on a
swallow. I must drop his quaint mispronunciation, to
make his meaning intelligible.

"It is all the same," he would say, "it is all the way
of nature. We men are but speaking brutes. Christianity must be trumpeted again through the world, and
again with miracles to support it. But perhaps it is
as it should be. The mint and the thyme give out their
perfumes only when bruised. Human hearts are the
stops and keys in the great organ of humanity; and
the deepest and divinest music comes not from the
weak notes that are touched with gentle fingers, but
from those that are fiercely trampled under the feet."

"But, Herr Messing," said I, "what of those who fret
the hearts of men with their fingers, or trample them
under their hoofs? Surely there is some divine
retribution to follow them?"

"Of that I do not speak," said the professor. "'The
drift of the Maker is dark: an Isis hid by the veil.'
All that I know is, there is no music in the world
without violence. The Æolian harp is a legend. No
harp will give its music until fretted by the fingers.

Do you see that sea ?" he cried, pointing with his hand across the waters that lay calm and sparkling in the clear light of a frosty winter morning. It was curious that all our little solemn conversations took place by the sea, which we both loved. "Would you be content to gaze on it for ever with the 'anerithmon gelasma' never broken; or would you prefer to see it sometimes lashed into fury, and toying with the frail works of men ?"

"I confess, Herr Messing," I said, "I would like to see a storm once and again."

"And when the billows lift themselves aloft," cried the professor, kindling, "and curve their hungry lips in foam, and fling their awful strength, crested with whiteness, against each other, and spread the broken and hissing froth far around on the green breakers, and scent the air with salt strength, and hiss at the wind that whips them—what would you call it ?"

"I'd call it very grand," said I.

"But suppose those green hissing waves happen to catch between them one of the frail works of men, and toss it from one to another in scornful play, and dip its prow and stern alternately in the salt spray, and with every blow, like a thousand Nasmyth hammers, shatter its iron plates, whilst the wind above tears its sails into pennants, and stately masts are shattered, and a few trembling wretches with white faces stare with every plunge into their graves; and the winds think no more of the little god of this planet than of an autumn leaf, and the sea no more than of a fragment of brown weed—what would you call it ?"

"I'd call it very terrible," I said, as the picture rose to my mind.

"Well, my friend," said the professor, relaxing, "you must have the tragic element in human intercourse, as in nature, to maintain the proprieties. There are even those who think life not worth a day's purchase if there were no excitement, and who would prefer the fierce tortures of anxiety to the dull pleasures of peace."

"That's all very well for the fierce and bold," said I,

"for warriors and sea-kings; but what of the gentle and feeble? Is there no protection for them?"

"Yes, there is," said he; "and there is just where our modern education is so defective. The ancient Greeks were more merciful than we, when they put to death their weaklings and deformed. We speak of our humanity in saving life—but for what? For a living death, to which mere death were a pleasure. We save them to be the sport of sin and injustice. Victims from their birth, they come into the world with an inheritance of weakness or of shame, and, miserable Ishmaelites, they walk the dark ways of life, the scorn of their kind, and the toys of destiny. They can no more help themselves than babes. They can no more rise than lead in the deep waters. And whatever Christian temples may be built, and nowever the name of Him may be invoked, whose birth was a shame, and whose death an ignominy, there is but one God worshipped to-day, and his statue is labelled 'Success.' And as at the sound of the sackbut and the symphony all were commanded by the ancient king to fall down and adore the golden idol, so at the jingling of the guinea the world falls down and adores its demigods. And as, when the gladiator fell in the Roman amphitheatre, every hand was raised and every thumb lowered to condemn the conquered wretch to death, so, when a poor fellow falls down weary in life's battle, there is neither pity nor peace for him. Your poor tutor won't easily get a place now," he continued. "If he had the good sense, as the world calls it, to issue a mighty prospectus, and sign himself Alfred Bellamy, Esq., with a string of letters after it, and dress decently, and get over his stammer, he might have the pleasure of knocking dunces' heads together for a few years more. But as he is only a scholar and honest, he must starve."

"But you spoke of a remedy in education, Herr Messing," I said; "what is it?"

"Oh!" said he, "it is a fancy, a dream, a chimera.

You will laugh when I tell it to you. I think our whole system wrong. It is not education at all. It is filling in, not drawing out or developing. It is making the human mind an arithmetical, or geographical, or historical calendar or register, that may be used by the Government or individuals, as a typewriter or self-adjusting thermometer is used; but the higher faculties —the soul itself—alas! alas!—Would you tell me (I am following the example of Socrates) what is most required in war, or in difficulties political or personal?"

"Well, I suppose," said I, "courage, prudence, and self-reliance."

"Very good," said Herr Messing. "Now, tell me what is most required in times of tranquillity—say for the State?"

"Good government, I presume!"

"And for the individual, what is the best thing in the world—better than wealth, better than honour?"

"I suppose inward peace, and peace with all men!"

"But to secure that peace, what is necessary?"

"I really don't know, Herr Messing," I said. "Most people think it comes with the attainment of some object in life"—

"That is," said he, "with the acquisition of wealth, beauty, power, etc.?"—

"Yes," said I.

"How does it come with these?" he said.

"I suppose desires are satisfied!" I answered.

"Are they?" said he. "Was there ever yet a man satisfied with the possession of what he desired? Alexander with new worlds to conquer, Mark Antony tired of Cleopatra, Napoleon, even at Austerlitz, dreaming of his First Communion—no! no! Peace comes not with the fulfilment, but with the quenching, of desire. Self-denial is the watchword! A man must be superior to his circumstances. They are fleeting: he is immortal. They are valueless: he is above all price. Peace, divine peace, comes only when man has ceased to wish. I had rather be a Socrates with his one garment and a meal of olives, than Alcibiades with his purple and high feasting. So thought Alcibiades himself, when he took off his crown and placed it on the head of the sage. And who would not prefer to die as Socrates did, in the glory of his prison, than as the young prince in all the infamy of a lupanar? But all this is philosophy, and philosophy is out of fashion in our schools. It is preached in the churches; but in the churches men lose their five senses. They do not see the collection-box when it is put before them; they lose the sense of touch of the dear little coins in which they wash their hands during the week; they do not hear the clergyman, except when he makes a mistake. And in the schools, as we know, everything is taught but the divine accomplishments of self-knowledge, self-respect, and self-reliance. Given these things, and something more sacred—of which I do not speak now—man is master of his fate, and the weak are more powerful than the mighty, and wrong and injustice fall as harmlessly as the waves on these rocks. Steeped in the peace of the stars, the world spins round them, and they look on as silent spectators in calm and repose."

He was silent, looking out over the curling waters; but I broke in—

"But won't that theory destroy all ambition? and what is man without some ambition?"

"Yes," said the professor, "it does destroy ambition for questionable advantages; but it does not exclude the ambition for perfecting oneself in all those things that make man like unto the archangels. There are two classes who stand aloof from ordinary humanity by their service to man's two great glories—the mind and the soul. Saints and thinkers stand out from the dark mass of ordinary humanity, as clearly as a priest from his people, or a warrior-general from the dark files of his soldiers. It may be that they have walked their exalted way alone. Without irreverence we might say, 'Their way is on the sea, and their pathway on the

deep waters, and their footsteps are unknown.' But
when they pass, men begin to wonder, and from wonder
they pass to praise, and from praise to worship. What
names are to-day most reverenced amongst men?
What names are imperishable, for they are written on
the deep heart of humanity, and not on the brittle page
of history? Why, the saints of the Church, and then
the kings of thought!—Plato and Aristotle, Shakespeare
and Bacon, Newton and Leibnitz. Just take their
histories and trace them! The poor pauper, who
breathes his last agonising sigh on the straw pallet in
the workhouse, was not more insignificant than they!
But they were happy—yes, infinitely so—loving life,
and not fearing death. And the little malice of men
broke harmlessly upon them, for their souls were on
high—with the universe—and 'man was a squirming
worm.' And I say all this to you, mein vrendt, that,
come what may, wrapped in the serenity of self-
reverence, you may possess your soul in peace. But,
mein Gott!" cried he, starting from his reverie, "it is
six o'clock, and the Grinder will be mad. And I do
expect some Christmas cards from Germany these
days."

CHAPTER X

AT YULE-TIDE

"He wandered day and night. To him both day and night were
    dark ;
The sun he felt, but the bright moon was now a useless globe.
O'er mountains and through vales of woe the blind and aged man
Wandered, till He that leadeth all led him to the vales of Har."
                  W. BLAKE, *Tiriel.*

THE days had shrunk into a few short hours of rain
and gloom, and the darkness had lengthened into long,
long nights of weary hours and dispiriting sadness. The
long lines of street-lamps sent their blear light through

6

murky fogs as early as four o'clock in the afternoon ; and we, without the comforts of warm, well-lighted dining-rooms, and the snug luxury of happy homes, hid ourselves and huddled together in the study-hall, with its musty smells of ink and books and paper. There, during the long, dreary afternoons of the Christmas holidays, we spent hours together, toasting bread and nuts, and singing, and telling such wonderful tales that the *Arabian Nights* became tame by comparison. We had a glorious stove, which was always on the point of being red-hot; and around this we clustered, and beguiled the weary time as best we could. The Count was generally away on long rides these dark days ; the tutors were all at their homes ; the Grinder had gone away somewhere; and ours was Liberty Hall for a short season. During these days, Coulette, otherwise so uncompanionable and unsocial, became our mainstay. Sitting opposite the stove, smoking little cigarettes, with his feet propped up on the ledge of the stove, when it was not too hot, he sang for us, recited long pieces of poetry, and, a prince of raconteurs, told us story after story, that, inasmuch as they could not be true, showed wonderful powers of imagination. These stories he varied by snatches of sea-songs, which he had picked up either at 'Frisco or on his voyage over to Europe. His favourite song was the " Fairy Bell," for which the Grinder, to his own discomfiture, had reprimanded him. Another was a sailor-song, the burden of which was—

> "Bony went to Moscow !
> A heigh—ho !
> Bony soon came back again !
> Jean François ! "

and he had all Dibdin's committed to memory, from

> "Here, a sheer hulk, lies poor Tom Bowling,"

to the

> "Good little angel that sits up aloft," etc.

He could bear no interruption, however. He should be allowed to sing all his songs just as he pleased, and

in the order he pleased. The moment he was interrupted, tortures would not drag another note from him.
One thing seemed to concern him deeply these days—
and that was the absence of the Grinder. "Where had
he gone? Would he return? When *will* he return?"
—these questions were put every day regularly, and
with an anxiety that was quite inexplicable.

"You appear to have suddenly grown fond of him,"
said Cal, who was privileged.

"Perhaps I have reason," he answered.

But one of his many stories was so pathetic and
mournful, that it clung to my memory, whence many
other more remarkable things are erased. It was
an old tradition, not so old as to be beyond modern
sympathies; and Coulette privately assured me that
it was no invention of his own, but it had come
down from one or two past generations, and was well
authenticated by reference to some old papers which
were kept in a safe in the little church at Santa
Barbara.

THE LEPER OF THE PACIFIC COAST.

"I have amused you so far," said Coulette, "by
telling you of vaqueros, carboneros, arrieros, aguadores,
and cargadores. Listen now to something more grue-
some. Some fifty years ago there was a young lad
living at a certain fishing station along the Pacific
coast. For convenience sake, I shall call him Diaz.
He was passionately fond of the sea. He used sit for
hours on a grassy cliff overhanging the blue Pacific
waters, or lying at length on the yellow sand, doing
absolutely nothing, but watching the long waves roll in
peacefully and break amongst the pebbles. When he
grew older, he became a boatman and a fisherman; but
he always went out alone. He could not bear company
of any kind. Night on the waters—the moon shining,
and his long lines trailing along the deep—this was his
home—he wanted nothing else. He used go pretty far
away from the shore; but no one minded. He used

remain away for days together ; but no one seemed to
care.   Storms are unknown on that coast, and the
dangers are few.   Diaz was a dreamer, but not a
coward.   What he was doing all these nights alone on
the deep seas, I cannot conjecture.   I should have slept,
or gone mad.   Now, there are one or two dangerous
currents along the coast, rather far out from land.
They move up along the coast from Nicaragua and
Panama, close to the land ; then they fan out widely,
and drift dangerously to the sea.   You can almost see
these inter-oceanal rivers running rapidly onwards and
outwards, and corks, melons, decayed leaves, débris of
every kind floating rapidly to mid-ocean.   One night
Diaz, I suppose in his sleep, slipped into one of these
currents, made a frantic attempt to recover himself,
slipped his oars, and was carried out to sea by the fatal
current.   It was moonlight ; and he saw no hope.   He
had a few fish caught.   This was his chance of life.
He drifted all the weary night towards the mid-deeps.
Then, I suppose, tired of watching, he fell asleep, and
dreamt of Santa Barbara.   He awoke, to find his boat
tugged violently aside with a boat-hook.   It was the
dim dawn ; and, leaning over into his boat, he saw, not
the sweet face of the saint, but such a face that he was
absolutely paralysed with terror.   The head was grown
to treble the ordinary size ; the hair had fallen away as
if it had been singed ; the eyes, browless and without
lashes, were sunk deeply in caverns of swollen and
putrid flesh ; the nose was eaten away absolutely, leaving
the two triangular apertures into the skull ; the lips
were destroyed, leaving the hideous teeth bare ; and the
wretched swollen and distorted frame was naked to the
waist.

"'O Christ!' was the exclamation of Diaz.   He rubbed
his eyes, thinking it was a hideous nightmare.   No!
the awful figure threw itself back into the stern of
the boat, having his own fast by a rope, and pulled
with long and steady strokes away from the track of
the sun towards the shore.

"Stealing an occasional frightened glance at the terrible face, Diaz crouched in the bottom of the boat, wondering what was the meaning of this new and dreadful experience, and clinging to the one hope that they were steadily nearing the land, and there would be a hope of rescue. But when the sun was high in the heavens, and a faint blue mist of shore deepened into the placid form and outline of hilly land, Diaz saw with sinking heart that this was not his home. It was a strange, beautiful country; but it was not his. In a little while his eyes were dazzled by what he thought steep, high banks of crystal clouds, through which the sun made wonderful and dazzling pictures. It gradually dawned upon him that they were the white billows of mountains, stretching north and south, far as the eye could reach, in one unbroken but serrated undulation of radiance and brilliancy, and he saw for the first time the Sierras. Then the demon who held him prisoner, laying down his oars, buried his face in his hands for a while; then, covering the hideous lineaments with a white cloth, he spoke, and his voice was a voice as of falling waters at night, or as a far-off cry coming piteous and mournful as from a fallen angel from his bed of pain.

"'You fear me, and you hate me,' it said, and Diaz wept to hear it, 'but perhaps you will yet pity me and love me. You will know what I am, but not yet. You must only know what I shall do. I am taking you to the sweetest spot on all the marvellous Pacific coast. You shall have all things that man's heart may desire —only do not hate or shun me. I will give you wealth beyond all dreams and expectations; servants shall do your bidding; you shall have horses to ride, boats for the open sea; the mountains are full of game, and my men are skilled hunters—all, all shall be yours, but do not hate me, do not shun me; do not hate me' —his voice faded away into a broken murmur, and he bent his head lower, until his forehead touched the thwarts of the boat. The boy's mind was agitated by all kinds of ideas and sensations—wonder and regret, pity and repulsion; childish delight at the anticipation of what was coming, dread of terrible possibilities; a feeling of exultation at the free, joyous life before him, and a sense of depression at the thought that he was, after all, but a captive, and his jailer was a ghoul and a monster. Then he thought he should say something.

"'I know not who or what you are!' he cried. "I was dreaming of my saint when you came to me. But I know you have no right to make me your prisoner, and take me from my home'—

"'Your home was on the great deep,' said the sad, muffled voice; 'you were lost, and I—even I—saved you.'

"This was a thought that had not occurred to the boy. He did not feel he was rescued, but captured.

"'I had not thought of that,' he said, with more compassion. 'You have saved my life, and bought my freedom.'

"'But you are not my slave,' the figure replied. 'You are my friend, my child. If you had been fond of home, I would not have touched you. If you had been wound up in parents, sisters, or friends, I would not have asked you hither. But you have been as solitary as I. Your home was on the deep seas. You have had no friends but the winds and waves—no companions but the stars. What have I taken from you—in comparison to what I shall give? Look!'

"They were close to the shore—no sandy parterre, glistening with pebbles and shingle, but one rich glowing mass of foliage down to the water's edge, where the shadows shone black and lustrous in blue transparencies. Far as the eye could reach, the deep, green, trembling clouds of leaves in summer splendour rolled billow after billow, until they were lost in the glittering background of mountains, that shone with apocalyptic splendours in the rosy light of a brilliant sun. 'How and where can we land?' thought Diaz, when, as they skirted this wilderness of trees and shrubs, an

opening was suddenly made; and the figure, still
muffled, guiding the boats safely, they glided into deep,
still waters, green and pellucid, so that the smallest
pebble could be seen at the bottom, and the branches
swept them as they passed between, and creepers struck
their red and golden blossoms into their faces, and they
rowed in silence through narrow channels, overhung
with the twilight, and filled with odours and perfumes
that made the air heavy and faint after the bracing,
biting salt air of the sea. Along these narrow channels
they passed, the blue-green water never for a moment
becoming shallower, but sometimes expanding into tiny
lakelets, where the strong sun made a furnace of the
air, then narrowing into straits, cooled and darkened
by the shadows of the shrubs and creepers. But there
was no joyous animal life there—no bird to make
colour amidst the sombre verdure, or song in the solemn
silences; but once or twice a long, lithe snake swung
from the branches, swaying his painted and mottled
body to and fro, as if he would dispute their passage;
but, after looking for a moment at the white-veiled
figure, he would draw back, frightened or abashed, and,
coiling his smooth body around a branch, look long and
wistfully after the boats. At last, and when it had
seemed to Diaz that they must be now miles from the
sea and close to the radiant mountains, the veiled
figure stood up, whilst the boat slowed down and
stopped, and, standing to his full height, he drew off the
embroidered veil, and said—

"'Look at me once more! You snall not see my face
again, unless you shall try to escape me!'

"Diaz looked long and steadily with a look of fascination at the awful face and figure, and noticed that the
fingers of each hand, with the exception of the thumb
and forefinger, were destroyed. Then the figure, drawing a valise from under the thwarts, began to clothe
himself. He drew over his naked and disfigured body
a chiton of red silk, that closed around the swollen
neck, and was clasped by a huge brooch of solid gold,

in the centre of which a large ruby burned. This garment draped the whole figure. His arms were left bare, but at the wrists were bracelets of solid gold, marked with white stones, framed into curious letters. Then over his head he flung a white veil—not what he had first worn, but one of far richer material, and embroidered with gold lace, sewn here and there with garnets and emeralds. No aperture for eyes or mouth. Blank darkness! But the strong, muscular arms gripped the oars, and, without turning to right or left, sent the boats through a narrow shallow into deep water. Then, brushing swiftly through a curtain of matted creepers, they burst into a lake, the wonders of which took the breath away from the boy, and made him gasp and choke with fear and delight. For all around that wondrous sheet of water, where the sun slept, and stars looked at themselves at night, the same thick matted foliage crept down and rested on the water's edge, save in one place, where there sprang into the sky a marvellous palace—such as set men dreaming in the white city of the Adriatic—glistening in white marble, bastioned and turreted aloft in the blue sky, with deep windows embrasured here and there in its white face, and in other more favoured spots, great oriels overhung the still waters, and swayed and trembled in their shadows, as the boats swung to anchor beneath them. A broad flight of marble steps, to which beneath the lip of the waves the purple seaweed was clinging, swept up to a portico pillared and panelled with alabaster and mosaics, and standing there the sad figure beckoned to the wondering Diaz, and said, 'Come!' The boy leaped lightly from the boat, ascended the steps, and followed his captor into the hall. Here new wonders awaited him. Great palms swung their feathers high as the lofty panelled ceiling, and, between them, lofty fountains threw their silver spray into the air, and statues of glistening marble crouched, or slept, or watched their shadows in the deep basins of the fountains. Diaz followed his host from room to

room, from wonder to wonder, until at last they came
to a little chamber that overhung the lake. Here the
great figure, in its rich garment of red and white, flung
himself upon a couch, and said in a weary voice, ' You
must be tired—eat!' And Diaz ate and slept, and
slept and ate, for many days, the same figure always
watching and waiting, never touching him with his
hands; and dumb servants waited on him, and antici-
pated every want, and kept every shadow of annoyance
away from him. And somehow, as the remembrance
of that dread face and figure faded from his memory,
not being renewed by daily observance, the pity in the
heart of Diaz grew to a kind of love for this nameless,
solitary being; and, after some time, he no longer
shrank from him, but awaited his coming, and showed
by a thousand little gestures how much he appreciated
his kindness, and how tender and compassionate he was
towards his suffering benefactor. Yet he knew he was
a prisoner in a gilded cage. The servants, always
polite and deferential, deftly evaded every curious
question he put to them as to the personality of their
master, or the locality in which they lived. Once, and
once only, they answered him straightly, when he
asked how far they were from the sea.

"' That is the sea,' they said, pointing to the lake.

" He looked puzzled.

" ' Taste and see,' they said.

" But when he explained that he meant the open sea,
they told him it was five miles distant in a straight line
—twenty or more by the channel they had traversed.

"' And the woods?'

"' The woods are impassable, owing to the thick
undergrowth of creepers and the knotted roots of
fallen trees; and they are alive with serpents and
poisonous insects.'

" This cut off all hopes of escape, and made his deten-
tion all the more irksome. Were he an easy-going,
phlegmatic lad, he might have resigned himself freely
to his imprisonment; but the fact that he had been

deprived unjustly of liberty, even though his captivity
was so pleasant, made life almost intolerable. From
that day he ceased to take pleasure in all the pomp
and splendour and luxury that surrounded him; and
he spent his days, and a great part of his nights, in
devising means of escape. With this feeling came a
kindred one of violent repulsion to the strange being
who had seized him, and to whose happiness Diaz
would now appear to have become essential. For
though his friend and captor rarely spoke, Diaz felt
his eyes watching him with infinite kindness and
solicitude; and if every precaution was taken to prevent his escape, so, too, every precaution was taken
to save him from the slightest inconvenience. One
thing struck Diaz in after life—that his strange host
never touched food in his presence; and that the air
of this wonderful sea-palace was impregnated with a
strange, powerful, pungent odour, that was made
tolerable only by the sweetness and scents that
breathed from the glorious flowers with which the
mysterious dwelling was literally filled.

"Many months of this gilded captivity had rolled
by, when one day Diaz wandered far towards the
mountains, through thick copses of undergrowth, where
roots were twisted and matted together by tendrils,
and the great arches of the trees shut out almost every
gleam of sunlight. At last, after much trouble and
fatigue, he reached an open glade, green and tender
with young grasses. He dwelt long and earnestly and
lovingly at the little picture of fresh nature hid in the
sombre majesty of the woods, when, turning suddenly,
his eyes caught a glimpse, far away over the broken
lines of shrubbery and foliage, of the shining and
trembling sea. He shook with emotion. There was
his beloved ocean, shimmering and glinting under the
glorious sun; and, far away, on the dim, straight line
where sky and sea touched, a few white sails shone
like stars, and spoke ineffable things to him. All
the old love of his heart came back—all the myriad

memories of his boyhood. Days in which he slept on
the bosom of his great mother—nights that were filled
with waking dreams of stars and shadow-stars amongst
the wastes of waters. He thought he smelt the whole-
some breath of the sea, and felt its bitter touch stinging his cheeks into unaccustomed blushes. He stretched
his hands towards it, and wept. He looked down
towards his white prison, and almost cursed it. He
had become feeble and effeminate amidst its unwhole-
some luxury. He loathed its heavy-scented atmosphere, its luxuries, its quietness, its solitude—above
all, the hideous spectre who had brought him thither.
Then a thought struck him. He would cut his way
to the sea. But the woods full of snakes? He had
encountered none as yet; and, in the name of God, he
would make a struggle for life and liberty.

"For two days he laboured and toiled towards the
sea. On the evening of the second day he emerged on
a beach, his clothes torn in shreds, his face and hands
scratched and bleeding, his whole frame tingling with
pain, and weakened by hunger and toil. Here he
rested during the chill night. In the morning a fleet
of fishing-boats appeared in the offing. He feebly
signalled to them, and they put out a boat to rescue
him. But lo! as they shot out again from the beach,
and made for the fleet, three or four boats, well manned,
drew out from the thick copses that sheltered the
shore a mile or more to the south, and Diaz knew he
was pursued. Fortunately, he had gold in abundance,
the free gift of his benefactor and jailer. He urged on
the lagging boatmen with promises of reward, if they
reached the fleet in time. They put out every effort,
and Diaz lent a strong and willing hand at the oars.
But his heart sank when, as the other boats narrowed
the distance between, he saw the familiar figure in
scarlet and white standing in the prow of the leading
boat, and making frantic gestures to his men. Then
it became a race for life or death. But the fishermen
of the fleet perceiving that it was a chase, and thinking

that perhaps Indians manned the pursuing boats,
hoisted sail and bore down on the unequal chase.
Then the pursuers slackened their efforts. But the
great massive figure, raising himself to his full height,
put his two arms high over his head, and, without a
word, plunged headlong into the sea. They could see
his men craning their necks over the sides of the boats
to mark where he fell. But he never rose again.

"Diaz told his story to the fishermen, and saw them
look anxiously at each other. He told them of the sea-
palace and its untold wealth, but they shook their
heads gravely.

"'Not for worlds would they approach it.'
"'Why? What superstition was this?'
"'It was infected.'
"'And he?'
"'*Was the famous Leper of the Pacific!*'

"It was coolly debated in his presence whether Diaz
too should not go overboard. But he proved that he
was clean, and his appeal to Santa Barbara saved him.

"Ten years later, master of a Pacific fishing fleet, he
ventured up the narrow channel to the hidden lake
and its palace. All was ruin! The palms had out-
grown themselves, and projected their leaves through
the broken windows. Slime and seaweed soiled the
white marble approaches, the walls were rent in some
places as by an earthquake; and when Diaz, guiding
his boat to the old landing-place, was about to step on
the marble stairs, two fierce snakes coiled to strike,
and shot their quivering tongues towards him."

A few nights after, just at the close of our Christmas
holidays, the Grinder returned, much to Coulette's
delight. I knew it by the strong smell of creosote in
our corridor, and by the death-bell, cough—cough—
cough—heard throughout the night. Verily, if the
coral insect can build up reefs of adamant on the
Australian coast, there are often more minute microbes
that can sap and destroy the masters of creation.

"What would you have done if you had been in the place of Diaz?" I asked Coulette the following morning.

"Driven a stiletto into the leper, and taken his place in that glorious palace."

"But the leprosy?"

"Bah! no fear of that. I'd have washed myself every morning in eucalyptus, and laughed at the danger of infection."

The Count came in to our entertainment the last evening of our vacation; and, without a word of preface or explanation, he lit a cigarette at the stove, and told us the following experience.

CHAPTER XI

THE COUNT'S STORY

" A bow, a touch of heart, a pall
Of purple smoke, a crash, a thud,
A warrior's raiment rent, and blood,
A face in dust, and—that was all."

IT was day certainly, because up in the rifts of clouds you could see the faint splendours of the sun; but darkness, as of twilight or eclipse, was over the city, from huge clouds of smoke that rolled in in heavy masses from the south-west, where the public buildings were on fire. I could scarce see the white face of my father, as he lay on his deathbed in a large room in a quiet street on a slight hill that overlooked the city; and when I opened the window shutters, I could see the thick vapour scudding over my head, as you see clouds crossing the moon on a wintry night; but in the heart of the vapour were red sparks of fire, and occasionally burning flakes of paper, or other light material, would fall gently on the window, and leave a sooty mark behind. Once I flung open the sash widely, but shut it promptly, for the room was choked by the smell of burning petroleum. The silence of the room was unbroken, save by the heavy, laboured breathing of my father, and occasionally by the light footfall of mother or sister, who would approach the bed to soothe him. Then again stillness, but for the heavy breathing, or the tick of the clock on the mantel-piece.

"How do you feel now, dearest?" said mother, on one of the frequent occasions when she had to wipe the death-sweat from his brow.

"Better," he said gently; "but, Marie, it is dreadful to die without the Sacraments."

Mother was weeping softly, but tried to console him.

"Well, dearest, the *Bon Dieu* will supply all. From Him the graces of the Sacraments come, and He will do all that is required for you at the supreme moment."

"Mother," said I, turning suddenly from the window, "father must see a priest. I'll go for one."

"Nonsense, child," said my mother; "you'll go to certain death. Besides, where can you find a curé now but in prison?"

Father looked wistfully at me.

"I'll go, mother, whatever befalls."

"Let Henri go, mother," said my sister Emmeline "God and the Holy Virgin will protect him."

I kissed them all tenderly, and, gliding down the stairs, I opened the front door and looked out. The street was deserted, the houses shuttered and closed as if death were everywhere, and the sound of my footfall clanged and echoed as at midnight. I kept close to the wall, as I hurried along down the steep, and across the streets. I stopped before the little church of Notre Dame de Lorette. It was closed. I knocked loudly at the house close by; but the clangour that I awoke in the street alone answered me. Still through the silent streets I went, great billows of smoke rolling over my head, and the awful crackling of burning buildings in the distance, until I came to the Church of St. Eugene.

Again I thundered, and even kicked the door in despair; for the further I advanced, the more difficult became my task and my return. Again I woke empty echoes; but an old beldam, putting out her grizzly head from a street close by, asked what I wanted.

" Monsieur le Curé," I said, " for a dying person."

" Go home, child," she said, not unkindly ; " Monsieur le Curé has to shrive himself just now."

My heart was sinking as I glided along, until I came straight before the spires and pinnacles of St. Eustache. And I prayed with all my heart to the martyr in that hour. Then I passed around the building, keeping carefully hidden by buttresses and niches, and knocking here and there gently, for some great fear was upon me. I had passed round the church, and turned the last corner, when I came face to face with a veritable soldier of the Commune. Tall and scraggy he was, and black, with a fierce beard that covered his face. He had the *bonnet rouge* on his head, and a long rifle leaned against his shoulder. He stood silent as a statue when I almost fell against him, and he smiled when he saw my terror.

" Not a young petroleur ? " said he; " you would hardly have been afraid of a citizen-soldier. You are white enough to be an aristocrat."

" I am not an aristocrat," said I boldly. " I am the son of a soldier of France, who is dying, and who seeks the ministrations of religion. Over his bed are medals of Alma, Magenta, and Solferino."

" Ha! ha!" he cried; " then he was one of those wretched mercenaries who sought to stifle the liberties of a brave people under the tyrant MacMahon! You have spoken badly, my young friend. Come with me!"

I reasoned and expostulated. In vain. MacMahon was already shelling the outposts of the Communists from Mount Valérien, and I had confessed that my father had been an officer under MacMahon.

He called to an ill-looking ruffian to take his place, and then led me right through the *Halles Centrales*, past the Church of St. Germain d'Auxerre, across the *Pont Neuf*, and into the Cathedral of Notre Dame. He was accosted by the shrill cry of " *Qui va là ?* " from a *sans-culotte* who ate oranges near the door, and we passed into the magnificent basilica. I had seen it but once before, when my father took me to hear a celebrated preacher; and all I remembered was a sea of heads, and a great voice reverberating through the building, and a sigh from the multitude when he had done, and the buzz of criticism as the multitude passed through the doors. Now, all was changed. And if I did not know the famous basilica, I should nave imagined that the markets had been transferred here from over the river, or that this was a barrack, and a very disorderly one. For the floor was littered with dirty straw, and horses fed from holy-water troughs, and hideous men in hideous apparel were eating or smoking on the benches, and dreadful language and blasphemies filled the air, and a monstrous figure was in the famous pulpit, declaiming unspeakable blasphemies to " *Mes chers frères.*" Within the sanctuary, whither I was led, a number of Communists, probably twenty, were seated round a sanctuary table ; but their looks of scare and anxiety contrasted strangely with the ribald merriment outside. Maps of Paris covered the table, some coloured, some white; and one of this motley council had a pair of compasses, and was measuring, or pointing out to his comrades some place of retreat or defence, if it became necessary. They looked up as my captor led me to the table, with—

" *Un prisonnier !* "

" *Sacré !* " cried the leader, whose name was Ranvier, "what have we to do with prisoners, when at any moment we may be prisoners ourselves ? Take the brat away !"

He turned anxiously to the map again ; and, whilst he turned, a shell came crashing along, and, striking one of the small pinnacles of the temple, sent its iron fragments dancing on the roof over our heads.

"Getting hot," he cried impatiently. Then, with a scowl, "We'll have our revenge!"

A courier came in.

"Well?"

"Thirty of our brethren shot by the Versaillais in the Parc Monceaux!"

"For what?"

"They were *pompiers*; it was found that they were pumping petroleum and hot water on the burning houses in the Rue Royale."

A shout of laughter greeted this announcement.

"Brave fellows!" said the president; but his brow darkened as he spoke.

Then, suddenly turning to me, he said—

"Here, boy, is a message! It is nearly time, brothers, is it not?"

"It is time," said they, rising.

He came to where I was standing, and handed me a parchment document well sealed. He bade me take it to the Pantheon, ask for the commandant, and give it to him, and "Mark you, boy, your life has been spared just now; keep a whole skin and do what you're told."

I had no alternative but to comply; and as I passed down the aisles the scoundrels were up and alert, looking to their horses and rifles, and the fierce ribaldry had given place to anger and fear. No wonder. For nearer and nearer came the crash of musketry, and the screams of the shells over our heads. Just before us the Hotel de Ville was blazing merrily, and up along the quays we could see in the air the mighty volume of smoke and the cloud of sparks that shot from the burning Tuileries. Hither and thither, now, as the troops came nearer, girls and women went raging through the streets, pouring petroleum everywhere—down through the cellar lights, through ventilators, through gratings,—their faces alight with the fury of the fire and the fierceness of their passions. Every report that came was a source of additional fury; for they were told that no quarter would be given by the troops, but that every

7

citizen caught on the streets, whose hands or clothes
smelt of powder or petroleum, was instantly shot. And
above their curses and shrill laughter was the roar of
the flames as they crept up the pillars and façades of
the public buildings; and through the noise of the
flames pierced the sharp patter of the bullets, and the
shriek of the shell, and the rapid rolling of the
mitrailleuse. An immense crowd was gathered in front
of the Pantheon, whose magnificent dome rose high and
clear above the smoke and flame that were consuming
Paris. And every fierce passion that could degrade
humanity, and deform the faces of men, played on the
countenances of soldiers, women, and children that
were gathered there. But above all was that fiendish
pallor that appears on the faces of those who contemplate
some mighty crime, and are determined to accomplish
it, although the consequences may be fearful to themselves. On the broad steps of the temple, surrounded
by a crowd of Communists, the commandant was giving
final directions. Some common movement impelled the
crowd towards the east; and they filtered away gradually
towards the École Polytechnique, and I could now see
Communards stationed with lighted matches at different
points of the square, and the truth flashed suddenly
upon me. They were going to blow up the Pantheon.
Deep in its vaults they had heaped up barrels of gun-
powder, and these sentinels were to light the trains that
led to the vaults. I had no chance whatever of approaching the leader, but stood transfixed near the famous
Bibliothèque that faced the temple. Then came a
rumbling sound, that soon became clear to the ear as
the tramp of armed men; and in a moment the word
was given, the leaders fled, the trains were lighted, and
I could see the little red jets running along the ground
and converging towards the door of the great temple.
I had realised the fact, terror-stricken as I was, that in
a few moments that dome would be lifted high into the
sky, and the Pantheon would be riven asunder, and half
that hill, with all its splendid buildings, would be

shattered as by an earthquake—when, leaping like
maddened tigers into the square from the deep mouth
of the Rue Soufflot, came, with level bayonets and blazing
eyes, a company of marines. I could see distinctly their
teeth hard set through open lips as they swept into the
square, and, tramping out energetically the smallest
spark of smouldering powder, they rushed on the mob
that was choked in the narrow lanes; and I could
just hear the muttered curses and the first thuds
of the bayonets as they crashed through clothes
and flesh, when I fell and was trampled, and knew
no more.

When I regained consciousness, the night was
struggling to the dawn; and when I had restored
circulation to my numbed limbs, and could look around
me, I found myself in a close room with about eleven
or twelve Communists, and then I realised that I was
a prisoner. As the dawn increased and morning came,
I saw that Fate had thrown me amongst an evil lot.
Two or three grizzled wretches, unkempt and unshaven,
stood up and stared savagely around them; a few boys
still slept on the bare floor; but a young girl, dark,
but with perfectly moulded features, sat up and leaned
against the wall, humming in a careless tone the
Marseillaise.

The moment she saw that I was awake, she turned
towards me, and said, in a mocking tone—

"Well, my white aristocrat, you hardly expected to
find yourself here this morning! You shall have a
pleasant breakfast—of lead."

I looked bewildered at her, and she exclaimed—

"Your piece of parchment is your death-sentence!
Whatever chance we may have, you have none."

I then remembered the order received in St. Eustache,
and my heart sank when I heard it was found upon
my person.

"Say your prayers, *mon enfant,*" she continued;
"in less than an hour we shall all be across the
borderland."

The *reveillé* then sounded, and in a few minutes the door opened, and we were ordered out. A court-martial was rapidly held, proof of our complicity rapidly given, and, with the remark from the senior officer, "Well-bred, too; what a frightful thing for such a young lad to be caught in such dreadful work!" we were ordered to instant death.

We were handcuffed two by two, and, guarded by a detachment of marines, we were marched quickly along the quays, across a bridge, and halted just in sight of the famous Obelisque Egyptienne. I did not know what life was until that moment. The morning had broken with surpassing splendour; and although a pall of smoke still hung over the burning buildings, there was a brightness and light around the black edges of the smoke, where the level rays shone through the vapour and gilded it. The bright river ran beneath, already crowded with boats and barges; the painted steamers were getting up steam for their journeys up the idyllic waters through the Bois, and farther into the plain wastes of the country; newsboys were shouting the news of our execution; bells even were tolling from churches, where *Te Deums* would be sung, after the morning Masses, for the triumph of the Versaillais and the destruction of the Commune—all was glad and bright and fair again, and for us it was in a few moments to be—the dark realms of death. Did I pray? No. You never pray when going to die. Pray whilst you live, if you pray at all. There was some slight delay, and a crowd was gathering. They stared at us: some cursed us; some pitied us; and I noticed that a few ladies in deep mourning, on their way to Mass at the Madeleine, looked shyly at us, and then turned away, in pity or disgust, I know not. You are surprised I made no defence. I could not. I was paralysed; and then I felt instinctively that my story would be laughed at. The orders were stern and unexceptional — anyone caught in a mob of Communists, or whose hands or

clothes smelt of petroleum or powder, was to be shot.
And I—what was petroleum or powder to a parchment
signed by the chief of the Communists, and ordering
the destruction of the Pantheon?

At last eight o'clock struck, and a young officer rode
up. I recognised him instantly as the son of an old
friend and army companion of my father's—the Comte
de Brignon. My heart leaped with hope, for he was
actually my sister's betrothed; although he had been
absent in Algiers many years, and I was so young
when he went away that he could not possibly recognise me. He ran his eye keenly along our faces when
the sergeant of the detachment handed him a paper,
on which were written, not our names, but our sentences. I thought his eye rested on me for a moment,
but the thought was delusive. We were ordered to
stand up, and put our free hands behind us. We stood
against the battlements of the quay wall. The officer
took his place silently at the head of the company,
and quietly gave the order to load. The men's guns
were breechloaders. The click of the little levers is
yet in my ears. They were ordered to present, and
Death looked into our faces. We stared at the round
black little mouths of the muskets. At that moment,
by some instinct or inspiration from my good angel, I
blessed myself. The eye of the officer was on me. He
stepped quickly before his men, came to where I
stood, and led or rather pushed me aside. I heard the
young girl hiss, "*Cochon!* aristocrat!" The next
moment there was a deafening crash, a blaze of light;
and when the smoke cleared away, and the burnt
cartridge-papers had fluttered to the ground, the
writhing bodies of my late companions were seen in
violent convulsions. The sergeant stepped forward,
and, putting a revolver to the head of each of the
wretched victims, there was an end to their agony, and
silence. A tumbril, that was in waiting, was filled
with the dead bodies, and rolled away. Then the
officer turned to me

"Your name?" said he.

"Henri de Charcosset," I replied.

He turned white, and, placing his hand to his forehead, stumbled up against the battlements.

"My God! what an escape!" he moaned.

Like a man in a dream, he listened to my story; and when I mentioned my sister's name, he faltered, and placed his hand to his forehead again. Then, as the bells were yet faintly ringing, he called a cab, and we drove rapidly to the Madeleine. Mass was just commencing. We knelt side by side in mute thanksgiving for mine and his providential escape; and I don't think I ever saw on the face of man such a look of rapt devotion. When Mass was over, we entered the sacristy, and briefly summoned an abbé to our dying father. The latter was happily alive, and received the last Sacraments of the Church. He died a few days after. In answer to all eager questionings as to my adventures that dreadful afternoon, the young Count would only answer, with a smile, "He was my prisoner!" They shall not know anything of my escape from an ignominious death until the day of my sister's marriage.

It was a pathetic little story enough; but Evans should break in upon the thoughtfulness that filled us all with the sneer—

"You ought to be fond of making the sign of the cross, I daresay. Now, you think it saved you?"

Henri took off his cap, which he wore at all seasons, indoors and out of doors, and placed it reverently on the desk.

"Yes," said he, with emphasis; "I have not the slightest doubt of it."

Then, as if the remark jarred on his quick emotions, heightened by the remembrance of what he had just related, he ran his fingers rapidly through his hair, and in a voice of forced calmness, said—

"I have no doubt whatever, in a religious community

like this, these external marks of Christianity should
not be held in high reverence. I have noticed that
you Irish " (what contempt he flung into the words),
" whilst continually boasting of your faith, and cen-
suring less fortunate nations, forget to practise its most
elementary, yet significant, ceremonies. You boast of
the antiquity of your faith, but you are ashamed of it.
Your semi-educated professional and middle classes
would be ashamed to be seen at a confessional; in
your hotels, not one in a hundred would dare make the
sign of the cross before meals; in your conversation,
the name of God is never mentioned, and religious
subjects are strictly forbidden; you pare down and
minimise the teachings of your Church to suit Pro-
testant prejudices. We, in France, are one thing or
another. We are infidels or Catholics. But you Irish
are such a race of abject slaves, that you cling to your
faith, because it will save your miserable souls; but you
are afraid to practise the duties of that faith, because it
might interfere with your miserable bodies."

" Now, Henri," said young Verdon, jumping up, with
a hot, flushed face, " you have no right to say such
things. Our people are faithful and good. You French
are apostates."

" Pitch into these Irish beggars, Henri," said Coulette,
who was pacing up and down impatiently; " someone
must tell them the truth. It is impossible to stand
their intolerable boasting. Give it them right and
left."

" I have only to add," said Henri coolly, " that, as a
proof of what I say, you have never produced but one
great Catholic layman, and—you broke his heart."

Harry Verdon, who was boiling over with the heat
of indignation, again protested; and, coming over close
to where Henri sat, he exclaimed—

" What do you know of us, Henri? For shame, to
calumniate us, of whom you know nothing! Indeed
and indeed," he said appealingly, " if you only knew
our poor people down in the west of Ireland—their

miseries, their sorrows, their patience—you would not speak as you have done. When I think," said the little fellow, choking with emotion, " of these poor, faithful people, living in their turf cabins, on Indian meal, trudging, barefoot, miles to Mass, ever so gentle, so patient, so fond of God, I—I "— Here he broke down utterly in a storm of tears.

Henri, whose back was turned to the boy, put back his hand and grasped him firmly, saying—

"Never mind, my little man; I retract all that I have said, for your sake. Stand up always like a brave fellow for your country. I am sorry for what I said. But this *scélérat*" (pointing to Evans) "provoked me." He lit another cigarette and left the room; and we all very soon, with different feelings, followed.

CHAPTER XII

THE IDES OF MARCH

"Remember March, the Ides of March remember!"
Julius Cæsar.

ALL this time his deep devotion to study was telling visibly on Charlie Travers. Never particularly robust, he showed signs of failing vigour that alarmed myself and Cal. Black circles were gathering around his eyes, already too brilliant; and there was a white colour on his lips and cheeks that told its own tale.

"This will never do," said Cal to me one day, as we walked up and down the ball-court. "He is failing visibly; and if that savage O'Dell gets into conflict with him now, he'll kill him."

"That doesn't trouble me," said I; " but will Charlie kill himself?"

For I had fully made up my mind that, cost what it

would, there should be no fight between Charlie and
O'Dell.

That evening, for the hundredth time, I spoke to
Charlie, begging him to discontinue his hard work at
any cost.

"But, Goff," said he, "you are working harder
than I."

"That may be," said I ; "but, look here ! Look upon
this picture, and upon that."

I held up his big dressing-glass, and surely there was
a contrast ! He looked so frail and white and worn,
against the bronze and red of my rustic face. I took
his hand in mine and pointed out the difference. He
sighed, and said—

"Quite true, Goff; but what will become of my examination ?" And then, after a pause, "What will
mother and Mary say ?"

I was about to utter some profanity, but checked
myself.

"What will they say ? I daresay, if they could
see you now, they would tell you pitch your examination to Old Nick. I don't mean that they would
exactly use this expression ; but they would tell you the
exact equivalent."

We walked up and down silently for a time. Then
he said, clasping his hands nervously—

"Do you know, Goff, I have been thinking for some
time that it is all a mistake ? Do you remember that
evening last October, when we read together that
extraordinary article of Carlyle's upon ' Work ' ? Well,
I assure you, it is not solely the ambition to succeed,
nor yet the desire of pleasing my mother, that has
made me work so hard all the winter ; but I have got
hold of that Gospel of Work, or rather that has got hold
of me ; and, mind you, I am quite convinced now that
life is worth nothing without work—that work is life,
and that everything else is death."

"My dear fellow," said I, "that is all right. But
you must never push things too far. Carlyle never

meant that you were to kill yourself, or make yourself an imbecile for life."

"Perhaps so," said he; "yet if I fail at my examination, it will kill me. Nevertheless, something tells me that there is a something wanting, too, in that Gospel of Work. Carlyle grasped only half the truth. There is another half, hidden away somewhere. I wonder shall I ever reach to it. If I do, I shall be happy."

"Come out, Charlie," I said; "we can always discuss these things better in the open air."

We walked up and down under the bare branches of the limes and elms, close to the boundary wall.

"Now," said I, "let us thresh the thing out. I say you must stop working altogether, or at least you must shut off steam, and creep on more slowly."

"Granted," said he. "But I have a trouble somewhere, just what I hinted to you now. And, alas! you and I are but boys; and there is no one here that we can consult on such a subject."

"Why not try Mr. Dowling?" I suggested.

"No use," said he, shaking his head. "All these teachers here are faddists. Each rides his own hobby to death. The most rational man in the house is the Grinder. But who could dream of consulting him on a delicate question like this?"

"Well, Charlie," I said, "there is some truth in that. But what exactly is your trouble? Out with it. There is nothing like letting in light on a cross question."

He pondered deeply for a few moments, his hands behind him; and then, throwing back his cap upon his head, he said—

"Of course, Goff, you'll laugh at me; but I can't help it. When I read Carlyle first, I felt as if breathing a new atmosphere. It was a novel gospel; and it had the effect of a powerful tonic or stimulant upon me. It was so far above all that is mean and mercenary, that it lifted me into quite new regions of thought and principle. I assure you, all my work during the winter

is due to that Gospel of Work. But whether it is
failing health, or some higher inspiration, I cannot help
feeling that there is something wanting in all this talk
about Work for Work's sake. I am not satisfied.
Surely we are made for something else."

Then it suddenly dawned upon me that Charlie had
a decided vocation for the priesthood, and didn't
know it."

"Look here, Charlie," said I, "you made a mistake
in coming here. You should be now half-way through
your course at Maynooth."

He shook his head sadly, and smiled.

"I used think so once," he resumed; "but I am now
quite satisfied on that point. There was a young priest
in our place who used stop me sometimes, and look me
through and through, and say, 'What's this I hear
about you, Charlie? Going to be an officer, and lose
your soul? A few years of doubtful pleasure, and then—
a useless life, and perhaps hell! Give yourself to God,
my boy, and you'll never repent it.' But you know
everybody used laugh at him, although we loved him;
he was so desperately in earnest. Yet his words are
always coming back to me, and I cannot shake them
off. But I know I shall never be a priest, and God
doesn't intend it. Is there no other way to do any
good in life?"

We reasoned and reasoned, I putting my worldly
wisdom and my scraps of philosophy against his lofty
and far-reaching ideals; until at last I silenced him by
quoting his favourite, and bidding him look to the
present, and let the future take care of itself.

Cal's concern, however, took a lower and more
practical turn. Mixing freely amongst the boys, he
had ample opportunities of hearing things that never
would have reached my ears. He hinted darkly more
than once of mysterious preparations for a fight that
were going on in O'Dell's rooms. He discovered that
the latter went through several exercises in the day
with Indian clubs, and had a bag of sand in his room,

which he pounded religiously to strengthen his muscles
Then allusions were frequently made to a great coming
event; bets were taken in the classroom; and more than
once Cal was invited to look at and admire the brawny
figure of O'Dell as he shuffled along the walks, his
shoulders high up, and with menace and determination
in every step and gesture.   Evans was his trainer; and
more than once he imprudently gave vent to his feelings
by gloating over the pallor and emaciation of Charlie,
and the splendid "fighting form" of O'Dell.

"He'll knock him over the ropes with one blow," was
his boast.

Curiously enough, I was so interested in my studies,
and in Charlie's health, that I did not attach any
importance to these bulletins of war-preparations which
Cal brought me from time to time.   The thing was so
monstrous and flagitious, that I did not believe it could
ever happen that, deliberately and in cold blood, a
challenge to fight could be issued by boys preparing
for gentlemanly professions.   But when I expressed
such doubts to Cal, he said, boy as he was—

"But you know, Goff, this is a matter of honour.
O'Dell was beaten last year by Charlie; and then and
there he gave a challenge for the same date this year,
which Charlie and we, his friends, gladly accepted.
What can you do? I'm sorry for Charlie, that he didn't
keep in fighting condition, instead of wasting his time
over these books.   I'm afraid Evans is right, and O'Dell
will kill him with the first blow."

February was passing away gently, like some timid
creature that was shy of her weakness between fierce
January and blustering March.   The days were
lengthening slowly but surely; the dark murkiness of
winter was yielding to the cold steel-grey skies that
mark the early spring; and here and there the favourite
of poets and of all who love hidden and modest beauty,
my little violets were hiding their purple leaves under
broad green canopies, and only betrayed their existence
by that exquisite perfume that is dearer to the world,

I believe, than all the Oriental splendours of colour and
perfume in June. Then gentle February, after one or
two warm showers of tears, made her bow and faded
away, and iron-grey skies and roads enamelled in steel
told us March had come. But what glorious walks
Herr Messing and I had along the sea-coast these iron
days! Charlie was too feeble, or too unwilling, to face
that fierce, scorching east wind, the terror of the invalid,
the delight of the strong. But we buttoned our coats
tightly around us, and, with heads bent to the blast,
we met and repulsed the angry forces of a gale that
was worse than fifty storms. How, for a mile or two,
the blood used to congeal in our veins, and we beat our
arms together to promote circulation; how the first
faint warmth would tingle in our fingers, and creep up
ever so slowly through our arms, until at last a healthy
glow would be diffused through the whole body, and we
would feel our energies flag, until at last we were fain
to rest, warm and breathless; how, on the return home,
we came more quietly, and had time to notice the
birdlings stealing twigs for the spring nests, and the
tadpole jellies by the roadside streams, and the black
buds full of life, awaiting the call of spring to burst
forth into verdant beauty—the cold grey sky so different
from October, the grey landscape all around, the silence,
the solitude, the loneliness of nature—all these things
the pedestrian knows well, and loves the features of this
hard and barren month for the knowledge.

The 17th March broke with all the signs of mid-
winter, except snow, and without a single indication that
spring was hiding near at hand. After Mass and breakfast, we gathered under the portico, and some boys
amused themselves by admiring the various forms into
which friendly hands had woven the national emblem.
Whether it was something in the air that predicted a
storm, or whether it was the demeanour of some of the
boys, which appeared to be singularly and offensively
exultant, I know not; but, as we stood facing the black
and threatening north, and chatting in groups about

indifferent matters, I had a feeling that something was
going to happen—a presentiment, hard to define, but
quite tangible and real, that this day would not pass
uneventfully. The feeling very soon took shape, for
in a quiet moment Cal pulled my sleeve and whispered,
"Look out!" I was at once on the alert, wondering
and speculating what was going to happen. I missed
Charlie from our group; and immediately all kinds of
horrible suspicions began to chase themselves through
my mind, when I saw him, looking even paler and
weaker than usual, rounding the corner, and coming
straight to us. , He was dressed in a light grey warm
suit; and as he came towards us, not with his old
elastic step and bright smile, but slowly and with eyes
bent on the ground, the tears came into my eyes, and
I could not help saying to myself, "He is a wreck."
But this soft feeling soon gave place to one not quite so
gentle.   For, as Charlie passed on a step lower than
that on which O'Dell and Evans and their *asseclæ*
were standing, the former, looking into vacancy, and as
it were seeing nothing, projected a brown stream of
tobacco juice over the face and clothes of Charlie
Travers. The latter took out a blue silk handkerchief,
and, though flushed to the ears at the horrible insult, he
passed gently by, and began to remove the ugly stain.
O'Dell, as if nothing unusual took place, continued
chewing the tobacco and looking into vacancy. In one
rapid moment the usual conflict took place in my mind.
But only for a moment. Reason, prudence, everything
timid or apprehensive were swept away under a torrent
of passion. In one rapid stride I leaped into the group
of miscreants, struck Evans with the open palm of my
left hand, and sent him sprawling. Then I tapped O'Dell
on the cheek. Even at that critical moment I could
notice the little boys cowering and shrinking and terror-
stricken; but my eyes were on O'Dell. The fellow
never pretended to notice me, but, with hands stuck
deep in his pockets, and the plug of tobacco rolled from
side to side in his mouth, continued staring at vacancy.

A second time I struck him, more smartly. The blood
mounted to his sallow features, but he never changed
his position. Then the devil entered in and took complete possession of me. Hissing "Coward" into his ear,
I planted my feet firmly upon the pavement, thrust my
two open hands into his neck, grasping his collar and
tie, and with one violent wrench swung him round, and
flung him panting against the huge oaken door. Two
little fellows who were nearly crushed by his weight,
fled away screaming. He rose up, and then for the first
time showed fight by making two or three desperate
lunges at me. I slipped aside easily, and avoided them.
And, to show my contempt for the fellow, I struck him
only with my open hand, and made his pallid face
crimson. After a few minutes his breathing became
difficult. He was a mass of muscle, without nerve or
wind. Then, to close the wretched business, of which I
was beginning to get ashamed, I caught him once more
as before; and, once more getting a steady leverage on
the ground, I swung him round and flung him from me,
his huge bulk tottering down the steps and across the
gravel walk, where he crashed into a clump of escalonia,
and fell senseless. I held in my hand, as trophy, a paper
collar, and a green tie with a huge pin in the centre.
I gave one look at my fallen antagonist, and then, with
feelings of unutterable self-disgust and shame, I hid
myself in the ball-court, where a good hour's brisk
walking hardly restored my composure. It was some
salve to remember that Charlie now was safe; yet, when
he came to me after a long interval, and held out his
hand shyly, and thanked me, I felt that the victory and
his safety had cost me a great deal.

But the old fighting spirit came back when, in the
afternoon, the Grinder sent for me. He commenced in
his usual sarcastic manner—

"So, Mr. Austin, you are turning this place into a
boxing academy?"

"No," said I stiffly; "the professionals, *your* friends,
have been in training for months."

"What do you mean?" said he sharply.

"I mean," said I, biting my words, "that all that is loathsome and wicked in this vile place, all that you have taken under your protection and patronised, have been practising for this event. I hope they are satisfied."

"You are complimentary," he said; "people flushed with victory usually are."

"I am truthful," said I, getting warm. "If you, or whoever has charge of this—this—Academy of all the Sciences, looked after the morals of the boys, checked the infamy of some, and assisted the better boys to weed out all that was disreputable and shameful, this discreditable scene would not have been enacted to-day."

"Then you think it discreditable?" he said, catching at my word.

"Profoundly so," said I. "It is most discreditable that I should have been called upon to do with my hands what you should have done by the powers entrusted to you."

"Well, I suppose," he said, shrugging his shoulders, "according to all school traditions, there must be a fight in every college."

"Not, certainly, in civilised colleges," said I, "or in colleges where any decent principles of morality were taught. If you, or whoever else is in charge of this establishment, had cleared this place of such miscreants as O'Dell and Evans a year ago, this would not have happened, and our lives would not have been a misery."

"You forget," said the Grinder, "that that would mean a loss of £250 a-year at least to us. And what would pay tutors' salaries and butcher's bills?"

"The respectable students who would gladly come here," I replied.

"Nonsense!" said he, laughing; "if all our colleges were weeded of their bad subjects, you should close up three-fourths of the schools in Ireland."

"I see, Austin," he continued, after a pause, "you

have become, as I foresaw you would, a dreamer. I knew Dowling would inoculate you with the virus of his philosophy, which is to study and starve."

There was truth in the remark, but I was not going to yield.

"I'll see, sir," said I, "at the examinations in June."

"You'll fail," he continued; "and I shall be sorry for it, because I like you. You are a poet, and there is no poetry in the hard facts of life. You are reading and devouring Æschylus, instead of minding your Greek accents. You are dreaming of writing Latin like Cicero, instead of studying commentators on Virgil. And that good man Messing has possibly introduced you to Goethe and his philosophy. Your examiners will know no more about Goethe or Schiller than about the craters of the moon or the spectrum of Sirius. You will wonder at their ignorance, and probably be indignant, but they hold the scales and the "Væ Victis." It is probable—I speak from experience—that Evans will succeed, dunce as he is, and you and Travers be thrown out."

Now this was too incredible; and I concluded that he was trying to annoy me, so I answered—

"If writing anonymous letters and slandering the innocent were conditions of success, Evans would take the palm from the whole school unquestionably."

The Grinder knew well to what I was referring; but, to my surprise, instead of being offended at my allusion, he shrugged his shoulders and moved away, saying—

"Well, good afternoon, Austin. Do you know, I am sorry you and I do not understand one another better. I rather like you." A compliment I could hardly return.

But there was another compliment which I gratefully received and warmly returned, when the Count, striding up to me after his afternoon ride, when I was walking alone under the leafless lime-trees, grasped my hand, and said, with emotion, "Tu es mon frère!" He

8

was usually so silent and undemonstrative, that I was quite taken aback, and murmured some reply. But he went on to express his feelings fully about O'Dell, and his emphatic assertion that such chastisement as I had most unwillingly administered was absolutely necessary, that gradually I resumed my feeling of self-respect that had been sorely wounded, and parted from the Count with the consciousness that I had been completely absolved.

CHAPTER XIII

THE FIRE AT THE ASYLUM

" Why burns the red light on the tower
  So brightly at this useless hour ?

      .   .   .   .

The red flames stoop a moment down.

They whirl, they swirl, they sweep around
With lightning feet and fiery crown ;
Then stand up, tall, tiptoed, as one
Would hand a soul up to the sun."

JOAQUIN MILLER.

IT was only a few nights after the event narrated in the last chapter, that I, being sleepless from much study, tossed and turned and invoked every tutelary deity to come to my assistance, and drown my senses in unconsciousness. I had counted the lonely tollings of the quarters from the great clock near, and had numbered the dismal notes which told of midnight, when my numbed senses were suddenly wakened by a bright halo of light which shone on the wall of my room opposite my bed. I had argued that the dawn does not break from that direction, and that it was rather early for the moon to rise, when a curious flickering roused me to perfect consciousness, and a noise in the air as if some destructive element was at work. I rose hastily, and looked out. Surely enough, there were yellow flames playing against the windows of the asylum opposite; and already black heavy masses of smoke went curling and heaving and spreading themselves away into the midnight sky. I would have given the alarm of "Fire!" at once; but just as I heard doors opening, and the whispered consultations of the boys, the strident voice of the Grinder broke in with—

"Keep to your rooms, every one of you. Let no boy leave the college to-night!"

He passed away. But the order was too much for boys already excited by the strange scene going on opposite their windows; and one by one we dropped into the lawn, and stood, terror-stricken, when now the terrified shrieks of the inmates broke upon our ears. All this time the fire was gaining a tremendous hold upon the building, and we could hear the crashing of falling timbers, the shouts of the assistants, and the shrill laughter mingled with screams of the dazed creatures, who ran from place to place, without discipline, and sometimes plunged into the very flames from which they were trying to escape. We bore it with curiosity mingled with fear for some minutes. Then the Count, turning to us, said—

"Look here! I can't stand this any longer. How many of you will follow me?"

We looked around for the Grinder. The coast was clear. He had disappeared. We gave a ringing cheer, and plunged down the slope of the lawn to the gate. It was locked and double-barred. The wall was too high to scale. We were in despair. We could feel the hot breath of the fire upon our faces; and many of us were coughing with the smoke, and rubbing our eyes. In this dilemma, O'Dell, who had just been roused from his heavy slumbers, for he was a great sleeper, came to our aid. By the light of the fire we saw him at the head of the lawn, which sloped down towards the gate, where we were gathered, trying to move some heavy object with his huge shoulders. We ran up to him,

and found him struggling to push an enormous iron
roller, which had been used in the tennis-ground last
spring, down the declivity towards the gate. His object
clearly was to drive the immense weight full tilt against
the gate, and shatter it. We hesitated at such a step.
But when he said, " Come on, cowards. The women
are burning whilst you are shivering," we flung ourselves on the big weight, and, partly by pushing, partly
by pulling, we got it under weigh. And, under the
direction of the Count, who shouted, " En avant, mes
braves," we rolled it down the hill at a tremendous pace,
until, within twenty feet or so of the gate, we let go, and
the huge weight crashed through the heavy woodwork
as easily as a gymnast in a circus passes through the
tissue-papered hoop, the iron bars and bolts snapping
like so many silken threads. With a wild whoop we
dashed into the asylum grounds, and, rounding the burning wing, came face to face with the doctor and some
attendants, who in the courtyard were tending the burns
and wounds of the rescued inmates.

" Just in time, lads," said the doctor gratefully, whilst
he put some oiled lint on the burnt arm of a poor lady ;
" a few of you look to the fire-engine, and lend a hand
at pumping ; but the more active will see to the fire-
escape, and get these poor creatures out of the left
wing."

The Count at once assumed command again, and
told off a detachment for pumping ; whilst O'Dell,
Coulette, Cal, and I ran to the escape. O'Dell was
detailed to the task of bringing down by the fire-escape
the creatures whom we would rescue. On account of
his great strength he was well fitted for this ; and he
did his work well and willingly. Whether it was pride,
or some better motive, nothing could equal the courage,
strength, and daring he manifested amidst these awful
scenes, working up and down the ladder with his unconscious, or sometimes troublesome burdens, and all
the time in perfect, dogged silence. We rushed through
the wards, and faced our work bravely. But it was

awful. The poor creatures—some laughing, some screaming—refused to leave, until by main force we dragged them from their beds and forced them to the window. One dark, foreign-looking lady sat up and sang in a high voice—the broken remnant of a once powerful organ—some *aria* from a long-forgotten Opera, and held up her hand beseechingly when we strove to lift her from her perilous position. We left her there, and dragged to the window other helpless creatures, whilst she, unconscious to all around her, made the roof ring with resonant, if not musical, notes, her most singular accompaniment being the boom of the flames, and the crackling of fallen timbers, and the shouts and orders from the yard outside. In the rush and hurry we had forgotten a small ward off the main staircase, which was more exposed to the fire than where we were working. We were apprised of its existence by a series of appalling shouts which now reached our ears, and which told too distinctly that the fire had reached its victims. We broke through with a rush, and came into a small ward, containing but six beds, two of which were already seized by the flames. Coulette dashed at one, and I rushed to where a young and beautiful woman was actually playing with the yellow spirts of flame that were lapping all around her. She, by some mysterious aberration, mistook them for gaudy ribbons, and was trying with her poor burnt hands to wreathe them in fantastic fancies around her neck and arms. She smiled at me when I dragged her out from the burning bed. The flames caught my coat-sleeve ; but I did not heed them. With the horrible smell of burning flesh all around, and the agonising cries, and still more agonising laughter of the poor creatures in my ears, I rushed across the room. Coulette had already rescued one, and had pushed her through the window to O'Dell, and I was carrying my curious burden across the landing, when I came face to face with the Grinder. He was stumbling and peering with his short sight in every direction, but he recognised me at once.

"You too here!" said he; "get back to the college at once."

Then occurred a curious scene. The poor burned creature I was carrying slid to the ground, and, with abject terror painted on every lineament, lifted her hands to the Grinder and begged and implored for mercy. He too was puzzled for a moment; but it would be difficult to say whether he or the poor patient was more terror-stricken, when, looking closer, yet recognising her voice more than her features, he passed his hand across his forehead, and said—

"You—is it you, Marcella?"

Then, as if to himself—

"My God, will my folly never cease to haunt me?"

But in a moment, by an effort of his strong will recovering himself, he turned to me and said—

"Austin, go back instantly, and take the rest of your comrades with you. I'll see to this woman."

For a moment I hesitated, for there was a look of agonising entreaty in the poor lady's eyes that almost constrained me to remain. But the remembrance of my former unhappy encounter with Hugh Bellamy decided me, and I went across the lobby into the next ward, which was now cleared of its inmates, and descended the ladder. Then, as the cold night-wind searched me, I discovered that my right arm was stripped to the elbow, and severely burnt. I was passing along without a word, when the doctor saw me, and guessed in a moment how I was suffering.

"My poor fellow," said he kindly, "you have not escaped. But you were all heroes to-night, and I suppose you would not be perfect if you didn't add suffering to labour. Let me put a little oil on that wound; and get in from the night-air as speedily as possible. Keep the burn carefully covered from the air, and I'll see you to-morrow."

I passed through the yard, and could not help noticing, even in my pain, the fantastic gestures and whims of the patients who were rescued. Most were laughing at the terrible scenes through which they had passed; some were gazing stupidly around them; and some, with a lingering trace of Eve, were arranging their hair in long bands, which they drew up and tied over their heads. And it was quite a pitiful thing to see, in the red light, long dishevelled grey locks, made scant by age and sickness, and the feeble efforts of these poor souls to keep up an appearance even in that dismal place. I hastened home; but there was no sleep that night. Between the pain of my arm and the nervous excitement, I lay awake till dawn. Nor could I dismiss from my thoughts that strange scene with the Grinder. Who was this woman, and what were her relations with him? His wife, driven insane by ill-treatment? His sister, abandoned like that other whom we had already known? Some ugly mystery there was surely here, which I would get Cal to unravel. But as dawn was faintly breaking, I heard the rumble of the fire-engines, and the steady orders of the officers, who only then had been able to come from the city. I slept and dreamed, and woke to find that we were all gazetted in the morning papers as heroes, and that I was a martyr as well. And next day, and for many days, I held levées in bed like a *grande dame* of the old régime; and great and gentle people came and went, until nearly all the manhood and boyhood were driven out of me, and I had to stand a little bitterness and jealousy from my comrades, who had done far more work than I, before I became a rough student again. But I put my private detective Cal on the track of the Grinder, on the trail of suspected evil I had found, and he followed it like a Sioux, until he found and tied together every clue, and came at last to the truth.

CHAPTER XIV

A SUBTLE REVENGE

"Nescis quid vesper serus vehat."
MACROBIUS.
"Thou knowest not what the late evening may bring forth."

"I SAY," said Cal, one day that he was lounging on my bed during my convalescence, "I think that fellow O'Dell was actually hoping that you had become a cripple."

"Don't say that, Cal," I exclaimed; "he has forgotten all about that unpleasantness. He was really a hero the night of the fire."

"He is a sullen, dogged brute," said Cal, who always spoke from experience—"a boaster and a braggart; but I must admit he has courage in cases like that."

"You don't think he has forgotten?" I queried.

"Not by any manner of means," said Cal, shaking his head ominously; "he doesn't forget, nor forgive."

"And he will take revenge?"

"Undoubtedly, if he dares."

I was silent for some time, for this was not reassuring.

"I have told him — not personally: I hold no communication with the fellow—but I have told him indirectly, that yours is a skin-burn, that your sinews and muscles are uninjured, that your biceps are as strong as ever"—

"Where did you learn those terms, Cal?"

"You know, Goff," said Cal musingly, "I have always two strings to my bow. If I fail as a sub-inspector, or in my preliminary, I shall be a doctor in three years; and then probably medical attendant in some local lunatic asylum. I have taken a decided fancy to lunatics since the night of the fire."

"You make things easy enough, old man," I said. "Perhaps the lunatic asylum won't offer, or perhaps"—

"Do you know, Goff," replied Cal, "I don't take things half as easy as you. Now, you are a good fellow, but you are an idealist"—

"Wh—what?" said I, in alarm. "Where did you learn such an expression, Cal? You must be reading novels!"

"I am reading novels," he replied imperturbably. "Where could I get my knowledge of human nature, if not from novels? What opportunity have I here amongst such commonplace individuals? And yet there are idiosyncrasies enough, God knows, if we cared to study them. Take Coulette, for example. A brown savage, only clothed. Fit for Samoa or Laputa; not fit for civilisation. Strip him, and paint him, put him under a palm-tree, and he would eat 'roast man' as easily as you would eat a sandwich. Do you know, Goff, he has a history!"

"Then why don't you make it out?"

"Slowly, slowly. Your native impetuosity is your ruin. You don't understand delicate operations which demand time and tact. I tell you he has a history. I tell you more: we are living within reach of a romance that would make a fortune for some of our novelists."

"Well, you are mysterious, Cal, and I am not curious. Hallo! where did you get this?"

He had coolly taken a roll of cigarette-paper from his pocket, and a tobacco-pouch, and was folding a cigarette with all the ease born of experience.

"This is a new accomplishment, Cal," I repeated; "how and where did you learn it?"

"Soyez tranquille! mon ami," he said leisurely, rolling the paper between his fingers. "You see I have learned French too, and from the same source."

"The Count!" I cried.

"The Count is a gentleman," said Cal; "perhaps, indeed, the only gentleman in this establishment. Gently, gently, Goff," he continued, in spite of my gestures of dissent; "I don't deny your merits at all— your *aplomb*, your *savoir faire*, et cetera—but there is a *sine qua non*—no, that's not it; an *il n'y a point*—no that's not it either "—

"Perhaps you mean *Je ne sais quoi*," I conjectured.

"I thank you, Jew, for that word. There is an indefinable something about the Count."

"There is," said I : " his countship and your snobbery."

"Now, you are wrong again, Goff," said Cal imperturbably. "May I smoke?"

"Yes," said I; "but everyone will know it is you who have fumigated the room, not I."

"All right," said Cal. "Now, I was just saying that there is an *esprit*, a *soupçon* of something really gentlemanly about the Count. You know I am an imitative animal. I copy all things — dress, accent, manner, deportment, even peculiarities. I nearly ruined myself by trying to purchase neckties like those marvellous ones which the Count wears. Then I thought I should like to have hands and a complexion like his. *Voila!* I spent a fortune on cosmetics, and began to smell like a hairdresser's shop. Now, this is my present vice. How long I shall keep it up, goodness knows. But, to do him justice, the Count snubs me!"

"Did you discover anything that would lead to a solution of the mystery of the fire?"

"Yes and no," Cal replied, smoking like a sachem; "but that does not interest me now. What interests me now is" (he spoke slowly, to emphasise his words), "that Charlie Travers is every day becoming more like a ghost, and that O'Dell is meditating revenge."

I reflected for a time, then my fury at such cowardice and treachery overcame me.

"I declare to Heaven," I said, "if he touches him again, I'll break every bone in his body."

I had risen in my anger; but the pain in my arm shot through me like an arrow, and I fell back helpless.

"There, now, *soyez tranquille*, take things philosophically, my dear fellow. But, mark you, if O'Dell tampers with Charlie again, he will leave this house in disgrace. I think even our authorities are disgusted

with the brute. But something is pending. When and
how I know not. Have you ever read Macrobius?
No! Neither have I. I don't know whether he was a
Greek, a Roman, or a Macedonian. I don't know in
what language even he wrote. But here is a line that
I, 'a picker-up of unconsidered trifles,' stumbled upon—

'Nescis quid vesper serus vehat.'

'Thou knowest not what the late evening may bring
forth'—with which admonitory sentence I'll take my
leave."

I lay awake that night, and several subsequent nights,
watching for the slightest sound that would intimate
an attack on Charlie. He used to come into my room
every day and remain chatting. There was a weary
look about him that was quite distressing, and I used to
remonstrate with him about his excessive application;
but he would only smile and shake his head. I gave no
hint of what Cal told me, but reminded him gently of
the necessity of locking his door at night, as some
depredations had been committed in the house lately.
A precaution which he neglected.

One morning, a little after breakfast, I was in my
room, and reading steadily at my table, when a tap
came at the door, and the Grinder entered. He said,
without preliminary—

"Your friend Travers has overdone it. He has had
a fit during the night!"

"Good God!" I cried; "you don't say so?"

"Yes," he said, rather kindly. "The doctor is expected
every moment."

"Is he unconscious?"

"Not quite, but raving and incoherent."

"May I see him?"

"Certainly." And he led the way.

I flung off my dressing-gown, drew my coat over my
shoulders, and followed the Grinder along the corridor to
Charlie's room. A servant was in attendance, who was
doing his best in an awkward manner to soothe poor
Charlie.

" Here is Austin, Charlie," said the Grinder.

The poor fellow stared at me wildly for some time, as if anxious, yet unable, to recall my features, and then began to sob—

" 'Twas no delusion, Goff, I tell you: *it* was there where Ned" (the servant) "is standing; and, my God, it was fearful ! "

" Something he thinks he has seen," whispered the Grinder.

" 'Twas all flames, like the Evil One," Charlie continued. " Flames in its mouth, in its eyes, in its hair, and flames flowing from its hands."

There was a tap at the door, and the doctor was announced.

The Grinder hastily went out, and held a hurried consultation, and Charlie took occasion to say, quite sensibly and coherently—

" Don't go, Goff; don't leave me ! "

" Never fear, old man," said I, " I won't leave you ; but, for God's sake, Charlie, put that horrible thing out of your mind."

The doctor came in, and looked very grave, seeing the worn cheeks and the big, bright eyes of Charlie. After examining his pulse and temperature, he kindly said—

" Now, tell me all about this thing."

Simply and plainly and coherently, Charlie told how, after a few sleepless hours the previous night, caused by his racking his memory over a Greek line, he had fallen into a deep slumber, when he was awakened by the stealthy opening of the door, and by a bright light that shone into the room. At first he thought it was some poor sleepless fellow that came in for companionship; for at that time all were working hard, and there were bad nerves amongst them. Then the door opened widely, and a horrible apparition presented itself. It was someone, very tall, and all in flames from head to heel. At this juncture the Grinder proposed that he and I should leave the room, as the doctor might wish to be alone ; but as I was becoming interested, and as I thought I saw a faint smile on the doctor's lips, and, above all, as I beheld a piteous look of entreaty in Charlie's eyes, I said quietly, "No, thank you; with the doctor's permission, I intend to remain." The doctor nodded, and then for the first time gave me a good long professional stare, and I remained. Charlie went on to say how dreadfully frightened he was— paralysed, in fact—when he saw the figure in flames, and how, gradually, he grew faint, and then unconscious; and "Oh!" cried the poor fellow, whimpering, "if it should come back again to-night, what shall I do? What shall I do?"

When he spoke of being paralysed, the doctor looked grave, and, bidding him sit up and stretch forth his right knee, he tapped it gently beneath the patella. The leg at once jerked at the shock, and the doctor was satisfied. He said a few reassuring words to Charlie, and then left the room, beckoning us to follow. His decision was prompt.

"Overstrung nerves—a practical joke—not to be left alone for a few nights—and removal home as speedily as possible."

At the word "practical joke" my heart gave a great leap, but by a powerful effort I restrained myself. Yet I hope, on the day of the Great Assize, I shall not see recorded against me the awful thoughts that came surging through my mind at these words.

"Perhaps, Austin," said the Grinder, as the doctor was leaving, "you'll see after these directions?"

"Yes," said I, between my teeth; "and after some other things also!"

CHAPTER XV

AN UNEXPECTED CHAMPION

Παισθεὶς ἔπαισας.	Struck, you struck ;
Σὺ δ' ἔθανες κατακτανών.	And you died, having slain ;
Δορὶ δ' ἔκανες.	And you slew with the spear ;
Δορὶ δ' ἔθανες.	And you died by the spear.

ÆSCHYLUS, *Sept. contra Thebes*, 961, 962.

CHARLIE recovered from the shock much more easily
than might have been expected. His natural elasticity
speedily restored his nerve-power, especially when it
was understood that the apparition was not super-
natural, but only that of an infernal spirit still in
the flesh. Our beds were removed into a large room,
formerly the library of the mansion, and here Charlie
and I remained until his friends should come to take
him home. Meanwhile the news of this cowardly
outrage had spread amongst the boys, and, to my
amazement, disgusted them. It was taking things too
far, they said; and there was a tremendous revulsion
of feeling even amongst the class that hitherto had
clung to O'Dell. Indeed, since March that hero had
doffed some of his plumes; but he had regained some
favour by his unmistakable prowess the night of the
fire. But this last cowardly attack, that sought the
night, not the day, and dreaded fair manly fight, and
slunk into chemicals for revenge, revolted even the
lowest and most churlish spirits, and Evans and
O'Dell were avoided.

A telegram was sent to Clare the morning after
this attack, and, unknown to Charlie, his sister Mary
was summoned. I dreaded the interview. She would
be shocked at the wreck in her brother's health, and
he might be ill prepared for such a meeting. But it
had to be done.

Meanwhile Cal and the Count were constant visitors
to us. I was agreeably surprised at the Count's visits;

for somehow we had not been intimate, though quite friendly. There was that curious shyness between us, that is more remarkable in boys than in girls. In some tacit way Charlie and I chose to be together; and Cal was drawn by irresistible attraction to the Count. But after this last attack on Charlie, the Count became quite friendly, was concerned a great deal about Charlie's health, and, in general, manifested a personal interest in recent events that was quite refreshing. The evening before Charlie's sister came, Cal was quite mysterious, hinted vaguely at discoveries, put on all the airs of a successful detective, and altogether was in high glee, perfectly self-satisfied, though, indeed, that was his normal condition. I was hardly surprised, therefore, when in the evening the Count came in. He looked quite sprightly and debonair; and, after a few desultory remarks, he turned to me and said—

"Cela est mon affaire."

I didn't quite understand. He explained that the solemn duty of taking satisfaction on Charlie's aggressors now devolved upon him, and that he was prepared to discharge it. How and when that solemn duty was to be discharged was to remain a secret. I had no objection, for I confess I had no desire to get into contact again with that savage O'Dell. Yet I considered it only just to remark, that the avengers should be sure of their victim, and should make no mistake about the midnight aggressor.

"It is all right, Goff," said Cal. "We know him."

Then we were treated to one of Cal's detective feats. It appeared that Cal had very little scruple in visiting people's rooms on business—"no real detective could be so squeamish," he said—and in the course of his observations he had ransacked O'Dell's limited library, mainly consisting of sensational novels, for a clue. He had been for days quite unsuccessful. At last he stumbled on a coverless, tattered copy of *The Cloister and the Hearth*, by Charles Reade, and, turn-

ing over the well-worn pages listlessly, he came across
a passage marked with blue pencil, which detailed
the escape of the hero from one of the many impossible
difficulties into which the author had led him, by
covering his face, forehead, hair, and hands with some
solution of phosphorus. In the night, of course, the
object was hideous and terrific. To such base purposes
is science used! There could not be a moment's doubt
but that O'Dell had done exactly the same thing to
frighten Charlie into epilepsy or insanity, and had
been only too successful. To make assurance doubly
sure, however, Cal and the Count had visited various
chemists' shops in the city, and had at last discovered
that Evans had purchased a large quantity of phosphorus at one of those establishments, for the ostensible
purpose of exterminating rats. My conscience was
satisfied, and I gladly left the task of retaliation with
the Count.

Next day Charlie's sister came. I was summoned to
one of the parlours to meet her. She came forward
quite frankly, and spoke as if we were old acquaint-
ances. She told me that, through Charlie's letters, my
name was as familiar as his own in their household. I
hardly looked at her, but I could see a strong resemblance to Charlie, only her face was more frank and
free—a gentle, handsome face, brown from sea and sun,
with a faint freckle here and there, and, instead of the
fair, delicate gold that curled on Charlie's forehead,
great clusters of rich auburn lay coiled and curled
across a brow broad and white, as if the star of an
archangel shone there. I told her all, and saw without sorrow the tears well into her blue eyes, and that
gentle feminine brushing away of them as if they had
no right to come, being unsummoned. Then she drew all
her strength together, and commanded her nerves to
do their work and sustain her, as we passed up the
long flight of steps that led to the corridor where
Charlie lay.

I entered the room first, lest the sudden presence of

his sister should give him a shock, and he looked up at me with his own bright smile, and pointed to the bed, as if to ask me to be seated. Whilst we were chatting, his sister entered quietly, and, without approaching the bed, looked with infinite affection and pain upon him. He started, and looked from his sister to me, and then, with a wild stare, back again to his sister; and I could see he was terrified, for the beads gathered thickly on his forehead, and he said, in a low, frightened voice—

"Goff!"

"Well, old man?"

"Goff, I'm losing my reason; God help me!"

"Nonsense!" said I, laughing; "what put such a fancy into your head?"

"I thought," said he, "that after you came into the room, another figure entered, like my sister; and I cannot get it from my mind that she is standing there, near the door. It *is* my sister Mary: I can see her dress and its folds, and her braided jacket, and her chain, and, as sure as I see you, I see her face, and she is weeping. Oh, my God! my God!"

His sister approached, and knelt down by his bedside, and stooped and kissed him in her tears. But he held back her face for a moment, looking ever so strangely and curiously at her; and then, when an inquiring look directed to me was answered with a nod and a smile, he put his left arm wearily around her, and then his right, and locked his hands tightly around her neck, and drew her face down to his, and murmured, "Thank God!"

This was no place for me. I went out, busied myself about other matters for a time; and when I came back, after half an hour, I could scarcely believe that this was Charlie. For he was sitting up in bed, looking quite cheerful and happy, and he and his sister were chatting about Bob the pony, and Rover the wonderful collie, and friends in Ennis and Eyrecourt, and the milkmaid Catherine, whom he had christened "Rufa,"

9

because her hair was red. And he was altogether so well, that, after a consultation, we agreed that he was to go home on the morrow.

"But the exam., Goff," he said again painfully; "how can I ever pass it?"

"No fear of that, Charlie," I answered; "a few weeks at home will brace you up, and we will face these old fellows at Burlington House together in June."

I confess I did not regard the project of parting with Charlie with much equanimity. We had grown into each other's feelings so much lately, and I had so completely severed myself from the friendship of the other boys, to find in him answering ideas to every fancy, whim, or enthusiasm of my own, that I felt I should miss him sadly, and be almost absolutely alone during the dreary time that would elapse till I saw him again. Of course I had Cal and the Count, and, above all, my studies, which were now pressing hard on me; yet I felt that I should miss the support I always received where the heart threw out its tendrils of affection; and how rude and unbending was the fate that severed me from my friend, when we could be most useful to one another.

It was therefore a joyful surprise to me when, the next morning, the Grinder called me, and told me it was Miss Travers' express wish that I should accompany her and her brother to Clare on this brief holiday. "And somehow, Austin," he said, "I think the sea-breezes and the slight relaxation from work will help you more than severe application just now."

I packed my valise rapidly; and, more gleefully than any boy home for the first time for his holidays, I accompanied Charlie and his sister to the terminus, and was soon speeding south, marking every spot of the landscape my memory held since last I passed that way.

CHAPTER XVI

BY THE SEA

"Listening their fear, I could not say 'Amen,'
When they did say, 'God bless us!'
But wherefore could I not pronounce 'Amen'?
I had most need of blessing, and 'Amen'
Stuck in my throat."   *Macbeth.*

A HIGH moor, broken with white, bare limestone and scrub, and cut sharply off by a line of sea, turbulent and angry, and with a white mist always over it, was my first glimpse of the landscape around Charlie's home. Savage grandeur, wild, untamed freedom of sea and sky, and all its savagery drooping down and entering into the spirit of bird, beast, and man—it contrasted strangely with the tame commonplaces of my own home. For I had seen Nature but as a pleasant child, always smiling in its mantle of green, with a flower here and there in its hair; and the winds in our soft southern climate were zephyrs, and even the fierce south-western had warmth and comfort in its moist breath. But here Nature was stripped and naked, and through its rags of ferns and mosses, its grey, great ribs of limestone shone; and if ever it dreamed of clothing itself in decent attire again, those angry storms would burst upon it, as a gipsy would tear decent raiment from her brown, naked children, and would buffet and chide it, and tear into shreds that tender garment with which the soft earth is ever striving to shelter or array itself. But most of all did I discern savagery in the sea. For whereas, on our southern shores, the waves creep in half apologetically, with a murmur, and break themselves gently on the white sand, and play with small rounded pebbles, and are never lifted into any but tiny cataracts; here, on this western coast, the long breakers seem to sweep as if having gathered strength all the stretches of the ocean from Labrador, and then,

in one huge deluge, they swing their gigantic weight
and bulk against the iron barriers, or low down on the
limestone shores; and there, meeting the first resistance,
they break their dense masses into columns, and the
columns are broken into companies, and the most
daring climb up the ramparts, and sweep them clean
of nest or seashrub, and angrily mount and pass the
battlements, and spend their ineffectual wrath on the
elastic turf that makes its hardy home on the summits.
And down on the low shore there is neither shell nor
pebble, but vast plateaux of naked limestone, jagged
and fissured, front the sea; and in the hollow caverns
under your feet you can hear the tumultuous cadences
of the waves, and on the surface are square, hewn rocks,
pitted and marked, that might have been playthings of
Titans of old, but now are only butts and targets for
the fierce artillery of storm and wave. What glorious
rides we had along the crests of those battlements, the
inky sea far beneath creeping on sand and shingle, and
hosts of sea-birds screaming and wheeling around their
nests in the rocks! The feet of our horses fell softly
and noiselessly on the velvet turf, and we drank in
health from the salt sea-breezes, which blew through
our hair, and crept beneath our garments, and lingered
on our lips, and would have made our eyes pained and
weary, but that we could ever turn away from the level
reaches and low monotone of the sea to gaze far inland
on plains of limestone, darkened here and there by
the sweetest pasture the kine ever mouthed or sheep
cropped; whilst some gaunt, square keep, a stronghold of
lawless days, broke the sky with its jagged lines of
ruins, and brought past and present together in a
history of sorrow—ruin on the one hand, and desolation on the other. But a charm in its solitude, and in
Nature's eternal soothing, that was more than com-
pensation for the vulgar din of cities, or the writhing
masses of humanity. We seldom spoke much on these
rides. Nature was speaking to us, and it was enough.
We rode for leagues together without a word, and then

we would fling ourselves on the grass, or sit in one of those natural chairs which the sea has cut in the shelving limestone; and, after our little lunch, we would sit and look out on the changeful and sparkling sea, sometimes forgetting that we were far from home, and that we should make speed to be in time for dinner. These were days, the memory of which clings to one for ever—bright, sunny days, when the sea was dimpled in a thousand laughing wavelets; stormy days, when the white sea-horses reared and bit at each other in useless fury far as the eye could reach; and, dearest of all, grey solemn days, when the light was hushed and still, and one could see the black silhouettes of headlands from the Twelve Pins on the Galway coast down to the ramparts of Moher, and, far south, the dim haze that marks the promontory of Loop Head, where the Shannon leaps to the sea.

On one of our rides—it was a gusty day, and yellow flakes of foam were blown into our faces by the saucy wind—we saw in the distance a figure moving rapidly towards us, and, like ourselves, breasting the gale. His head was bent down, and he walked quickly, the folds of a short cloak that covered his shoulders blown behind him, and his hands firmly clasped, as if disdaining assistance from walking-cane or umbrella.

"Here comes Father Aidan," cried Charlie, as soon as he had recognised him. "He'll hardly speak to me, as I have not called to see him."

As he passed us he looked up, and I saw a thin, worn face, blue-black where he had closely shaven, and two piercing eyes, with lights flashing intermittently through them—eyes that made you bend down your own instinctively, as if the sunlight had suddenly struck them. A tall, gaunt form was no ill assortment to such a face, nor a voice soft and cheery enough, but with a metallic sub-note, as if he could change it at once into a shrill trumpet. He did not recognise Charlie for a moment. Then he came round to his side, and said cheerily—

" Hallo, Charlie! I'm so glad to see you. Mother told me you were running down for a holiday."

"Yes, Father Aidan," said Charlie; "and this is the friend of whom you have so often heard—Geoffrey Austin."

He gave me one swift glance out of his black eyes, then shook me warmly by the hand, and said—

"Ah, yes, indeed, I have heard of him—working for the gold lace and epaulettes, too, I suppose?"

"Yes, father," said Charlie, "we are both West Britishers so far."

"Well, I'll let you pass now," said the priest cheerily, "because I shall probably see you this evening. Doff the white colours, Charlie," alluding to Charlie's paleness, "and put on the red and the bronze. You remember Horace and his holiday—

> 'Et rebus omissis
> Atria servantem postico falle clientum.'"

He passed on, and we resumed our ride, Charlie exclaiming, "A remarkable man, as you'll find, Goff, before we return."

And a truly remarkable man I did find him—one of those rare thinkers for whom Mother Nature frames a special mould, having tired of her common plaster-casts.

He said little at dinner, sitting silent, thoughtful, and observant; eating well, but carefully putting aside dainties, and touching no wine. But, after dinner, as we sat in the little garden, sipping coffee, I had a sample of the man.

The half-gale that was blowing all day had subsided, and the clouds that hung low and dark over the horizon were now looped up and held back, to show with all solemnity of contrasts the splendours of a dying sun. But he had drawn down into his glorious grave in the sea a soft mass of fleece which was now burning gold, and the rays of which shot up and tinged the edges of the cloud-curtains with the same blood-red colour.

Down in the east, the neutral sky was faintly tipped
with pink, which was fading slowly into grey ashes, as
the sun dipped deeper into the sea. But in the centre,
where the great god lay sinking to his rest, there was
an apocalyptic splendour of fire and gold, and great
flakes of yellow radiances, blended with scarlet and
purple, overshadowed the bright disk of the sun. He
blinded us with his splendours for a moment, then
plunged headlong into the ocean, and sent up into the
zenith, and all along the illuminated hemisphere of
heaven, long lines of light. These too faded rapidly
into purple and grey; the night came down, and one
bright star, hitherto eclipsed, stood out clear and re-
splendent on the battlements of heaven, and carolled
over the death of the departed king. ,

"God has given us a splendid display of fireworks
this evening," said Father Aidan, lifting his hat in
adoration. "Pity there are so few to witness it and
praise Him." Then, after a pause, he added, "Laudate
Eum, sol et luna; laudate Eum, omnes stellæ et
lumen."

"Many will have witnessed it, and not praised Him,"
said I.

"True, Mr. Austin," he said musingly; "it is a
pitiable feature of our modern life that no one dare
mention the name of God in society. Men blaspheme
Him, and many swear by that Name, which the Jews
never spoke or wrote through reverence; but to speak
of Him, or what belongs to Him, in ordinary society,
would be regarded as a flagrant breach of good
manners."

"Well, but, Father Aidan," said I, "I suppose there
is some constraint in this respect, because it would
look like an affectation of piety."

"And men are ashamed of being considered pious?"
he retorted.

"Well, I suppose so," said I; "but I regard it as a
kind of compromise."

"There now," put in Mr. Travers, laughing and

removing his long clay pipe; "I knew you would hit on the fatal word. You have waved the red flag before the lion, Mr. Austin. Good-bye till tea-time."

What had I said or done? I was not long left in doubt. For Father Aidan's eyes were kindling with a strange light, and his hands were clenching convulsively, and when he spoke, he spoke thus, and I dared not interrupt him—

"You have compressed in that word, Mr. Austin, the whole sad history of modern society, and the lamentable attitude taken by Christian men and women towards that world which Christ declared was His worst enemy. I think I am quite familiar with every argument that can be advanced in its favour. I know that every argument is suggested by our own apathy and weakness, and does not rest either on the word of God or reason. Not on the former, for there we have declared: 'He that is not with Me, is against Me; he that gathereth not with Me, scattereth.' Not on the latter, because all our experience is, that whenever and wherever we enter into a compromise with our enemies, they invariably come off victorious. To compromise is to yield. It may sound tolerant and liberal; but it is acknowledged defeat. And hence, in every department, the world is cutting its way deeply and more deeply into the hearts and minds of Christian people; and whilst they abandon themselves freely to its solvent influences, they simply think that they are progressive and advanced, and that everyone who would drag them aside from the precipice whither they are rushing is old-fashioned and reactionary. And if ever a man of God stands forward and preaches the eternal verities, they whisper his condemnation amongst themselves, and wish, in all charity, of course, that he were more prudent. Prudence! that vice of cowards! How men shelter themselves under that name, to conceal their pusillanimity! Where crime has to be condemned, vice reprehended, the wicked admonished, the weak warned, the erring corrected, and men's sympathies

and predilections opposed and thwarted for the common good, they, on whose shoulders the responsibility
falls, shrink in terror from the task, unable to face
the mortification of wounded pride—and absolve themselves from censure by imputing their cowardice to
prudence! It is not prudent to check the libertinism of
the great, to limit the licence of the press, to fling down
a barricade against the dictates of a false, because
irreligious, progressivism, to keep politics and that most
inflated of human frogs, the budding politician, within
the bounds of reason and law, to be able to say to those
who would sway the passions of the people, 'Thus
far shalt thou come, and no farther'; and, in a word,
to be manly and independent, indifferent to the *aura
popularis*, not seeking the vain applause of an unthink-
ing mob, and quite indifferent to their censure. Such
were the philosophers of old, from Thales to Pythagoras,
from Socrates to Zeno ; and such, in a higher sense, were
He whose name is above all names, and the apostles
who inherited His Spirit. 'Ye offspring of vipers,'
'Tell Herod, that fox,' 'Let him who is without sin cast
the first stone '—this is not the language of compromise
or prudence. I can imagine what a shout of execration
would be delivered if such were used about certain
public events to-day, and how good people would shake
their heads and deplore its imprudence. But I am
wearying you with such platitudes, Mr. Austin. We
may meet again, and perhaps be wiser."

Just then Miss Travers came out, and invited us to
tea. Father Aidan declined, and passed down the narrow
garden to his home. And Miss Travers must have
thought me a fool or mesmerised, for I couldn't shake
off some spell that was upon me, until we sat down
to tea.

"Well," said Charlie's father, "what do you think,
Goff, of Father Aidan ? "

"I think," I said, with a certain priggishness, which
was then growing upon me, "that he will knock his
head against a stone wall."

"He knows it," said Mr. Travers; "he has done so already. But he says that we must all have hard heads, and by a combined effort smash that stone wall to atoms."

"Does he act up to these principles?" I asked.

"So much so that he is now twenty years a curate, and declines to be a parish priest; he rejected a degree given him, *honoris causâ*, by Rome; he has been twice in jail for his people, and was once fired at and wounded by a gentlemanly miscreant, a Catholic whom he had publicly to rebuke. But come, the evening is fine, and I'll show you something."

Mr. Travers, I should say, was a Clongowes man, and, like all Clongowes men, at least in the old and leisured days of learning, a scholar. He was quite capable, then, of understanding and appreciating this singular and original character; and although he did not follow Father Aidan through all his principles, he was his fast friend in that best of friendships that is born of esteem. His house, placed on the very comb of a hill, faced the four points of the compass; but on the east it was protected by a fir plantation, and on the west its drawing-room windows commanded a splendid view of the sea. A flower garden sloped westwards down the hill, to the road which ran winding in and out until it was lost in the main street of the little village. We talked freely of Father Aidan as we descended, Mr. Travers being quite full of little anecdotes of his single-mindedness and simplicity, until we gained the village street, and passed the priest's house. A lamp was burning on the bare parlour table, the windows were wide open, and we could inspect the interior. There was little to be seen. A few heavy folios lined a small bookcase at the wall farthest from us, and over these was a Crucifixion, sad and terrible enough. A few chairs completed the furniture.

"The people say he sleeps on the floor, wears a hair shirt, and lives, like the Curé of Ars, on a little brown bread and three cold potatoes; but there are secrets of the inmost shrine, where even I dare not penetrate."

We passed along the village to where a broad concrete walk, protected by a new iron railing, forms a primitive esplanade for the summer visitors. We leaned over the rail for some time, looking down into the chasms of darkness that were made visible by the white line of waves far below. A deadly chill was creeping over my senses. I began to long for Mayfield and my Greek poets once more. This serious man, with his asceticism, his unworldliness, his mediæval gloom, was becoming rapidly a painful burden to me. I was crying for something more warm, more human, and making rapid picture-contrasts between my Greeks, with their warm skies, their theatres, their Olympian games, their orators and sages, and such a presentment of Christian teaching as Father Aidan afforded. Something equally serious, but, I hope, not so morose, was in Mr. Travers' mind; for he said, I thought gloomily, after a long silence, "Come now."

We re-entered the street, and paused before a rustic chapel.

"I suppose," said Mr. Travers, with his hand upon the door, "we ought not to enter. But we can keep quiet till the bell rings."

The chapel was dark as a well except for one red point of light, denoting the lamp which swung before the Blessed Sacrament. Nothing, not even the dim outline of the windows, was visible; but we knew, we felt, that someone was in the church with ourselves. We crept behind a pillar, and paused. A slight *susurrus*, or whisper, caught our ear. It was the prayer of a man whose soul was before its God. The voice was not raised; but it was intense in its suppressed vehemence. More truly than the people, carried away by the eloquence of Lacordaire, exclaimed, "Il voit Dieu! il voit Dieu!" might we, listening in the darkness with profoundest emotion, have said to ourselves: Now this is no conventional prayer or worship: this is the voice of a man in agony, appealing to the Supreme Powers to help, or guide, or relieve him. It was the tone, not the words, which came muffled to our ears, that betrayed the intensity of feeling. It is easy to know, when emphasis is placed on every word and syllable, how the heart feels. And here, with just now and then a stifled moan that seemed to make the red lamp tremble, was every word hissed out into the ears of God, as if in conjuration of the Most High—so emphatic, yet reverent, so pleading, yet so invincible, that surely, we thought, Heaven must bend down to hear such prayers, and darkness blend with darkness to conceal from angels' eyes that there is such agony unrelieved amongst men. Not then, but in after years, when the Sacred Writings were more familiar to me, did I distinguish certain words—

"Vias tuas, Domine, demonstra mihi, et semitas tuas edoce me."

"Dirige, Domine Deus meus, in conspectu tuo viam meam."

"Quare me dereliquisti? et quare tristis es, anima mea?"

"Thy ways are upon the sea, and Thy path on the deep waters, and Thy footsteps are not known. Make known unto me, O Lord, the way in which I should walk."

Prayers for light. "What is he contemplating?" I whispered to Mr. Travers.

"I know not," he whispered back. "He is in much distress."

"Let us come away!" I said.

"Not for a moment," he replied.

For just then the sacristy clock struck nine, and the chapel bell boomed solemnly into the darkness. From behind the altar a light appeared. An acolyte was lighting up the six tall candles on the reredos, and we saw, right in front of the altar, Father Aidan in an attitude of crucifixion, his arms stretched to their utmost length, his head thrown back, and his face uplifted to heaven. He remained in this posture a few

minutes, until the bell ceased tolling. Then, as the
villagers filed into the dim chapel, and took their seats
silently, he ascended the pulpit, and in a clear, resonant
voice began to recite the Rosary. Then, as if struck by
lightning, my vow over my mother's grave, my solemn,
awful promise, came back upon me. I heard the
rhythm of the voices no more. I was struck, appalled
at my own infamy. For nine months a thought of
God, religion, or duty had not entered my mind. I
was so engrossed in study, so rapt by the new pagan
world into which my tutors had led me, that I had
no room for a thought of God. And now, conscience-
stricken, I knelt before Him; and the murmur of that
prayer went humming, humming through my dazed
senses, whilst I could not utter one word. All I
wanted was to get away—away from that dark prison
of a chapel, away from that dreadful man, whose voice
rang through my soul like that of an accusing angel—
away from my own conscience, that kept accusing me,
and which I tried in vain to stifle. Alas! I did not
know, until after many years, that it was God Himself
that was speaking to me and chiding me. Nor did I
know that I was commencing the fatal experiment of
trying to do without God; nor did I know that, once
having drifted from His side, I should not return to
that safe shelter again, until I had walked through the
waters of tribulation.

After the Rosary, a choir sang the "Salve Regina" to
the old grand Gregorian tones; then we filed past
Father Aidan, who now stood in the porch, and
presented an "Asperges" to each as he passed. It was
quite dark; I tipped the holy water, blessed myself
shamefacedly, and, with a sigh of relief, went out under
the stars.

CHAPTER XVII

THE WAIL OF A LOST SOUL

ἀληθεύων ἐν ἀγαπῃ.

"Speaking the truth in love."

TWENTY times that night I started from my sleep, and twenty times I determined to seek Father Aidan in the morning, and, throwing myself at his feet, confess my prevarication, and beg light and strength to know myself. But when morning dawned, and the bright sun shone into my room, I cast every scruple to the winds of heaven, and determined to go my own way rejoicing. For I knew, if I consulted Father Aidan, with his stern, uncompromising attitude towards everything that interfered with the interests of an immortal soul, I should hear, "If thy right eye scandalise thee, pluck it out and cast it from thee"; and I was not prepared as yet to abandon my beloved Greek, nor even the hopeful prospects that spread out before me. I knew that my religious spirit was impaired; but I said, like a great convert, "Not yet! not yet!"

The morning post brought a letter from Cal. It was a history of the Count's dealings with O'Dell in pursuance of his scheme of retaliation. It would appear that the Count deliberately challenged O'Dell to fight, and, disdaining the British weapons which nature provides, gave him his choice of swords or pistols. O'Dell, terrified, tried to laugh it off, but in vain. The Count persisted. O'Dell, dreading the quick death of the bullet, chose the sword. Now, the Count had been taking lessons in fencing from some military men in Dublin, and was quite an adept at the science. What followed, Cal will tell.

"You never saw anything so amusing as the way O'Dell tried to wriggle out of the difficulty. But the

Count held him fast. O'Dell appealed to the Grinder.
In vain. Then the fatal morning arrived. We all
assembled in the ball-court, the scene of Charlie's
triumph. The commemorative inscription was still on
the wall. O'Dell and Evans came down late—the
former sea-green, like Carlyle's Robespierre, though I
don't agree about that shade of colour with the vener-
able Thomas. I confess I was nervous about the Count.
I was afraid the devil would put it into O'Dell's head
to make a sudden lunge, which might be fatal. But
Henri had reassured me. He would suffer no harm,
and do no harm. Henri came down late also, dressed
as if for a ball, with a tea-rose in his button-hole, and
the whole man well groomed down to the tips of his
fingers. He was as cool as a cucumber: though why
that villainous vegetable is called cool, I wot not. He
carried two rapiers—two murderous-looking weapons,
glinting and shining in the morning sun, and with
points like the sting of a bee. He laid them down on
the concrete, giving O'Dell his choice. Then he coolly
took off his coat, and laid aside his highly ornamental
cuffs. O'Dell took up the rapiers, critically examined
them, like any connoisseur, which made all the young-
sters laugh, tested the points, bent the swords into a
semicircle, etc., etc.; but I noticed his hands were trembling, and a few beads of perspiration shone on his
noble forehead. The Count looked on coolly, and waited
for his selection. Then O'Dell stripped, took up the
rapier, and I thought I read 'Murder' in his eyes.
They crossed weapons; and then, as I suspected, O'Dell,
drawing backwards, made a feint at Henri's face, and
then a fierce, desperate lunge at his breast. If he had
struck, Henri would have been a dead man. But he
quietly parried the blow—how, I am sure, I don't know;
and then came a—what shall I call it?—a coruscation of
light that bewildered and dazzled us all. Did you ever
read Thomas Hardy's description of Captain Troy's
play with the weapon? That's just it. All I could
see was—lightnings playing round O'Dell's head,

flashes and glints of fire here, there, and everywhere,
and, as a grand finale to these fireworks, we saw O'Dell's
blade whisked out of his hand, and sent flying like a
meteor out over the wall. The poor wretch looked as
if he were mesmerised. Whether the flashes of the
Count's sword were in his eyes, I know not, but he
was quite dazed, and did not recover himself for several
minutes. When he came to his senses, he found himself on his knees, with the point of a rapier at his
throat, just where I locate the jugular vein.

"'You promise to leave Mayfield in twenty-four
hours?' said Henri.

"No reply. The point of the weapon made a dimple
on O'Dell's neck.

"'You promise to leave Mayfield in twelve hours?
said Henri.

"No reply. The blade drew blood.

"'Once more—you promise to leave Mayfield to-
night? If you hesitate, you are a dead man!' The
warm blood was trickling down O'Dell's neck. He put
up his hand, and looked at the red smear.

"'I promise,' he said huskily, and, with the old shrug
of his shoulders, he walked away. There is some great-
ness about the ruffian—he will be a great pirate or
burglar yet. Then came the comedy. Evans' was
looking on, white as a ghost, at these proceedings.
But when the curtain fell, and we had given three
times three for the Count, Evans was much surprised
when the latter took him by the collar, and walked him
over to where his own coat was lying. Then, plunging
his hand into the pockets, he drew out a dog-whip—
but let me draw a veil over the sequel. Suffice it to
say, as we do in our essays, that the chemist who
supplied the phosphorus for Charlie got a larger order
for arnica and belladonna that afternoon. Evans departed that evening with O'Dell, and, strange to say,
without a protest from the Grinder, who is changing
much. The Count is a brick—a τετράγωνος ἀνήρ, as old
Aristotle would say.

"*P.S.*—When are you coming back; or, to use the more expressive terms of Herr Messing, who is inconsolable at your absence: 'When iz he gooming back from dot dom blace?' Good-bye! Love to Charlie.

"CAL."

That letter gave us food for talk that day. Night brought its own experience. It was quite calm when I retired. At midnight I woke from a deep sleep, to hear a moaning noise down where the sandbeds grew the sea-thistles. I thought it was the wind rising, just as the storm gathers away in the distance, and comes swooping down in a hurricane on house and tree. But no! the moan came nearer and nearer, not increasing in volume or intensity, but plaintive and sorrowful. Then it died away softly into the distance, and I composed myself to sleep, only to be again awakened by the same mournful wail, that came nearer now, creeping along the ground, rising to the windows, and whimpering and murmuring in a tone of infinite sadness around the sashes, high over the roof, back again to the windows, as if it were a lost soul seeking shelter from a pursuer, until at last it crept through the closed windows, and moaned and wept around my bed. I was rigid with terror, and the perspiration burst from every pore. I think I should have gone mad, for I was so paralysed I could not shriek for help; but then the wailing passed away, through the windows, across the garden, until it went out and was lost across the trackless realms of the sea. There was no more sleep for me that night. Three times that dreadful cry came up the hill, chilling and paralysing me, three times it died away over the deep. I knew it was nothing corporeal —it was some spirit in its agony; and, unaccustomed as I was to pray, I did whisper a supplication for that poor soul, and then wept at the thought of its agony.

"You're late, Goff," said Mr. Travers, in a bantering tone, when I entered the dining-room after a sleepless night.

10

" You haven't slept well, dear," said the kind mother.

" I had a curious chill," I said, by way of explanation; "I fear the sea-air has some strange effect on me."

Just then Father Aidan, very pale, and somewhat excited, came in.

" It's all over," he said.

" Is Costigan dead ? " Mr. Travers asked.

" Yes."

" And all was right ? "

He shook his head.

" These poor girls are in a dreadful state," he said, looking appealingly from Mrs. Travers to her daughter. " I never saw such utter sorrow."

" Mary and I will go over immediately," said Mrs. Travers. " Have a cup of tea, Father Aidan ; you have been up all night."

The tea appeared to choke him. He gulped it down, coughed, and went out without a word. Mary and her mother were silently weeping. I went out alone, to a perch I had found in a secluded place amongst the rocks and remained there all the forenoon, thinking of many things.

That evening after dinner I told my strange experience to Mr. Travers, as we sat in the little garden.

" It was the Banshee you heard," he said; "it follows that family."

Then, after a pause—

" Boys, you are young and inexperienced. Life lies before you, and your paths to choose. Take a lesson from what occurred last night. But for this, I would not mention it to you.

" Fifteen years ago, I knew Costigan well. He used to serve Mass here in our little chapel—a fine young lad, with infinite promise before him. His parents were ambitious for him. They thought of nothing but the Woolsack. He was to be a barrister, then a judge, then Chancellor. And as the Queen's and Trinity were the reputed avenues to such advancement, he was sent, quite young, to the Queen's College, Galway. What happened

there I know not; but after four years he returned,
remained at home, but never darkened the door of
the village chapel. He had suffered shipwreck of his
faith. All that zeal and prayer could do was done to
reclaim him, but in vain. Father Aidan M'Kenna strove
to bring him back, but failed. Then something occurred;
and Father Aidan was obliged to refer publicly to it.
From that day Costigan conceived the most bitter ani-
mosity against the priest. It is well known that it was
Frank Costigan fired the shot from behind the sand-pits
that nearly cost Father Aidan his life. His father and
mother died of a broken heart. His two sisters, angels
on earth, if there be such, have tortured Heaven to win
his repentance. In vain. He has lived as a bad
Catholic; he has died impenitent."

Mr. Travers paused for a while. "You remember,
Goff, a few evenings ago, Father Aidan's prayer for light
in the little chapel. Well, he was called suddenly at
ten o'clock last night to poor Costigan's death-bed. A
sudden heart attack, a relic of rheumatic fever, brought
the poor patient to the doors of death. I believe there
was infinite trouble in introducing Father Aidan to the
sick man's room. He refused positively to see him or
any other priest. The weeping sisters were distracted.
At last Father Aidan entered the room and approached
the bed. Costigan was propped up with pillows. His
first salutation was—

"'What do *you* want here?'

"His second word was an angry cry to his sisters—

"'Take that man away, and let me die in peace.'

"Father Aidan was not discouraged. He appealed to
Costigan, conjured him by all that was holy to save his
soul. The sisters knelt at the bedside and added their
tears to his prayers. He looked on sullenly and silently.
His end was visibly approaching.

"'You know how helpless I am,' he said, 'otherwise
this would not be.'

The grey shadow of death was creeping over his face.
His elder sister exclaimed—

"'Oh, Frank! for God's sake, one little word of sorrow or love!'

"'Oh, Frank!' said Alice, the younger sister, 'for our mother's sake, one word of peace with God!'

"Father Aidan placed the crucifix before the eyes of the dying man. He looked at it wonderingly for a moment, as if he did not recognise the figure; then he drew back, spat contemptuously upon the sacred symbol, and turned to the wall, and died."

Mr. Travers stood up, and walked away to the village, leaving Charlie and myself to our meditations. After a long pause, Charlie said—

"I wonder is Mayfield another Queen's, Goff; and are we drifting like Costigan?"

But I was in no mood for such reflections. I only said—

"When shall we be able to return, Charlie? You are decidedly better, and our work is before us."

He only sighed.

Before retiring that night, Mr. Travers said to me—

"You mustn't think, Goff, that it was from Father M'Kenna I got these particulars. They came from the sisters of the dead man, through my wife. She told me such agony as she witnessed was beyond all telling. Father Aidan will never speak of it, but to God in secret. 'He always speaks the truth in love.'"

Two days later, as we drove along the white roads on our way to the railway station, we passed by an old churchyard, in the midst of which were the ruins of an ancient Cistercian abbey, and a grand old yew-tree. An interment had just taken place. There was no sign of stoled priest, or the mourners that usually linger around a fresh-filled grave. Only two figures in deepest mourning hung around that sad sepulchre—one lay quite prostrate on the grave; the other, a fair, beautiful girl, lifted her red eyes to the skies. Beyond those fleecy clouds, that steel-blue firmament, her faith saw the Eternal eyes look down; and she thought she read there—what she never would read in the eyes of men—

some faint hope for the sad soul that had passed above the stars. I shuddered; and Mr. Travers, turning, remarked that I was chilled, and drew his heavy coat across my shoulders. But once or twice afterwards, as we drove along in silence, he looked away, and drew his hands hastily across his eyes; and I think I knew the reason.

———

CHAPTER XVIII

UNDER THE LIMES

"Young head time-tonsured, smoother than a friar's;
Boy face, but grave with answerless desires;
Poet in all that poets have of best,
But foiled with riddles dark and cloudy aims."

SKIRTING the wall to the left of the lawn as you entered Mayfield, a long row of lime-trees ran in a semicircle, touching the lodge - gate at one end, and lost behind the college on the other. They were the first to shed their thin silky leaves in October; and now, as June approached, they were putting forth their tiny white balls under the shade of rustling leaves, and soon these would develop into the fragrant spicy tassels that scent the air in the twilights of summer. It was a sheltered walk under those limes, though the westering sun sometimes beat hotly against the wall; and here in the May evenings, especially after tea-time, Charlie and I would walk, it being now quite understood that not even Cal or the Count should disturb us. What glorious evenings these were! and how the memory of them, in all their quiet, meditative beauty, comes back again across the troubled waters of my life, when other and more stirring events have long since passed into utter oblivion. Not once, nor twice, but a hundred times, has this one soft recollection haunted me, sometimes to embitter and create

regrets, more often to console—a soft, sweet picture
across the blurred and disfigured canvas on which my
life's history is painted. The smell of the spring
grass trampled by our feet, the rustling of the thin,
delicate leaves overhead, the setting sun lingering on
every little coigne and corner where it could rest for a
moment, the far-off bells of the city, the tram-cars
jingling into notice one moment and passing into an
echo the next, the shouts of the boys at cricket, the
falling of the velvet twilight, so soft and deep and
tender, and, above all, our whispered conversations,
as we discussed our futures and drew upon our fancies
to create fairy pictures for ourselves—all these come
back vividly and pleasantly; and why is it that it is
only Memory or Fancy can clothe this and similar
pictures with that halo and brightness that are for
ever vanishing when we touch them?   And what
wonderful problems Charlie and I discussed on these
summer twilights ! For now a very tender and gentle
mood had mingled itself with all that was boyish or
manly in his character; and although he lived in the
certain hope of passing the forthcoming examination,
and declared often that it would mean despair or
death to him if he failed, for his mother had set her
heart on his succeeding, still I could see how his
thoughts were constantly reverting to the idea that
was for ever haunting him—that this was not the end,
but that something higher and greater was in store
for him.   What that was he could but dimly fore-
shadow ; but I could see that religious instincts, and
the lawful ambition of advancing in life, were in
perpetual conflict in his mind; and that he somehow
cherished a hope that some day he would be free to
abandon himself to the contemplation, or the fulfilment, of those lofty and divine ideas that were now to
be regarded as harmless boyish fancies or delusions.
On a lower level, a sympathetic contest was waging in
my own mind—the desire to succeed at my examination and secure a competence for life, I shared with

Charlie; but in place of his transcendent ideas was
the lower, yet still honourable, ambition of being a
scholar, and exclusively a scholar. Where he put
religion, I put knowledge; and the canonised spirits
of faith who were beckoning him into their footsteps,
had their counterpart in my mind in the ghostly demigods of science and literature, whose lives, for the most
part spent in desolation and poverty, had an unspeakable attraction for me.

"Mr. Dowling thinks," he said one evening, taking
off his cap and running his hands through his fair
curls, "that my chances now are good. He looks
upon your success as certain. He thinks less study
now, and more air and exercise, would suit me best.
The overstrained bow, he says, loses its resilience, and
either snaps or becomes useless."

"I think so too," I rejoined; "your best work now
is to take long walks with myself and Messing. We'll
speak nothing but French or German, and you know
this will be important for our oral examination."

"Yes," he said, with some pain; "I believe that we
must ease off a little now. But suppose I should fail?
I am tortured by the anxiety not to fail, and therefore
to keep working steadily. On the other hand, I am
sure this would be fatal."

"There is no use in these forebodings," I said, pretty
sure of myself, notwithstanding the Grinder's predic-
tion. "To hope is to succeed."

"Yes," replied Charlie; "and then?"

"And then," said I cheerfully, taking him up, "and
then—a competence, a comfortable berth, honour, and
emolument. When you, Charlie," I continued, "are
over there in India, on the fair road to being Governor-
General, and I am in the fair way to become
Comptroller-General, I'll visit you. Let me see. You
have a glorious summer residence in Simla or Benares.
Palm-trees wave before your door; your wine is cool-
ing in Himalayan snows. Dusky slaves fly to do
your bidding; your name is all-powerful in Hindostan,

and you are quoted as a statesman equal to Clive or
Hastings at Westminster"—

"That is an unhappy allusion, Goff," said Charlie,
smiling.   "Hastings   did   not   find   Westminster
pleasant."

"Never mind," said I ; " 'twill do as an illustration.
But where was I ? "

"You were just flying between Simla and London,"
replied Charlie.   "But to be serious.   Do you remember
that bitter stinging sarcasm of the Count last Christmas, after he had told us his story, and that unfortunate
Evans interrupted ? "

"It is quite gone out of my mind," said I.   "What
was it ? "

He tightened his lips, as if the recollection cost him
pain.

"He said that Ireland never yet produced a great
Catholic layman but one, and she broke his heart."

" Extravagant enough," I replied ; " but how does that
affect us ? "

"I never told you, Goff," replied Charlie, blushing at
the concealment, " that I took him to task over it : with
what effect, do you think ? "

"Of course you routed him, horse, foot, and artillery."

"No," said he slowly, " but he routed me.   He said,
'Just name another,' and I couldn't."

"Let me see," said I, pulling out drawer after drawer
of my memory; "wasn't there Brian Boru, and Owen Roe,
and some others, who were Irishmen, Catholics, and laymen ? "—

"Yes," said Charlie; " but clearly you don't understand.   He meant great men, like Montalembert,
Chateaubriand, Ozanam, Count de Mun, etc., etc., who
in our day, at infinite hazard to themselves, have upheld Christian faith and traditions, and to whom it was
the master passion of their lives to extend the empire
of the Church, and build it round about with such
strong buttresses that all the powers of modern in-
fidelity should rage ineffectually against it."

"Whew!" I cried, looking dubiously at Charlie; "this is a far cry from Simla!"

He took off his cap, and began to twist it nervously in his fingers for some time. We walked more slowly. The boys had left their games: they could no longer see where the ball was pitched. The last rays of the sun had died off the slanting roofs, and the soft shadows of a summer night were closing in around us. We were steadily drifting out of sympathy with one another. New ideas, that were quite foreign to me at the time, had taken hold of Charlie's mind—fast and firm hold; and somehow—was it contempt, or was it lack of understanding?—I could not enter into his thoughts and feelings, and therefore remained silent. He was embarrassed, and continued nervously twitching and rolling his cap between his fingers; and I thought I saw something like a twitching of the lip, or a more wistful look than usual in his eyes, as he said—

"I daresay, Goff, I look to you as weak-minded, or, perhaps, hypocritical. But I must say what I have to say. You know I'm discontented and unhappy. I am in search of something, and I cannot find it. I have work to do, and I don't know what it is as yet. But I want to be something more than a pleasure-seeker, a mere epauletted doll. Somehow, dimly, I perceive that my work is cast here at home. There is great need of zealous Catholic laymen in Ireland. The people are not rising up to the level of their great vocation as the Catholic nation of the West. What a glorious destiny it would be to lift them higher and higher, until the world once more wondered at them—to make them a nation of saints and scholars again! I don't mean scholars such as we," he continued, raising his hand as if to ward off an objection, "but I mean real scholars, who would pursue learning for learning's sake" [I most cordially agreed with him], "and then would consecrate their intellectual gifts to the glory of the Author of all knowledge, and the extension of His empire upon earth." [I did not understand this language.] "And oh," he continued, now quite kindled into enthusiasm, "if ever the day should come that I, lifting up my voice, could wean my young fellow-countrymen from their West-British ambitions and desires, their Civil Services, and snug Governmental sinecures, and concentrate all their energies in building up a great Catholic nation— Irish in its traditions, Irish in its sympathies, ay, even narrow and insular so far that a wall of brass would be builded around the island to keep out British ideas and principles, and those *fin de siècle* fancies that are steadily undermining religion amongst us—then I think I could sing my *Nunc dimittis* with resignation, ay, even with pleasure. And if, O good God! the day should ever dawn when the old monastic spirit would creep back into the land, and the now barren valleys of Ireland would blossom with cloister and choir, and the now silent skies would echo with the lost and forgotten art of praising God through the Church's offices; and if once more the children of the Church throughout the world would send their sons to us as to the central sanctuary of faith and knowledge—would not this be the realisation of all that the human heart could expect, and would not life be pleasantly sacrificed if consumed in such a glorious enterprise? But, but," he said. placing his hand to his forehead—

"You are speaking an unknown tongue to me, Charlie," said I coldly, but kindly. "I have not got the key, and I am mystified."

"But you *will* know it one day, Goff," he cried passionately; "we shall separate on this question one day, but we shall meet again."

The night had now come down, purple-black, and the summer constellations were rising above the horizon. Sun after sun rolled into its place in the firmament, until the dark background was pierced with points of light innumerable. The night wind rose and vexed the silken lime leaves; and a great bat flew round our heads and whirred away into the blackness. The air grew chill, and I proposed to Charlie to go in. He misunderstood my silence, and begged me to say something. I had nothing to say. Was I annoyed? No. Was I offended? No! What then? And I could only say, "I don't quite understand, Charlie; I don't quite understand."

He pressed me further for an answer, until I got quite angry, and forgot myself so far as to say—

"You have been bitten by that mad priest down in Clare, Charlie, and he has inoculated you with the virus of his own ideas."

He was silent, because I had pained him deeply; but he only said gently—

"Then you think Father Aidan really mad, Goff?"

"No," I said, with a shamed face, "I know he isn't mad; but—but he is unreal, unpractical, and he has made, or is making, you the same."

"Perhaps so," replied Charlie; "but I wonder is this the folly that is wisdom before God?"

I did not answer. We went in from the chill night air.

CHAPTER XIX

HARD WORK FOR LOST TIME

"O Life! O Time! ye were not made
For languid dreaming in the shade:
Nor sinful hearts to moor all day
By shady isle or grassy bay,
Or drink at noontide's dreamy hours
Sweet opiates from the meadow flowers."
FATHER FABER.

As a black cloud charged with lightning comes down on the brow of a sullen mountain, and rests there until, with flash and reverberation, it breaks into white cataracts, so gloom, deep, dark, unrelieved by one single ray of hope, seemed to have settled down on the sombre

countenance of the Grinder. We noticed the change
immediately after the fire at the asylum. He became
quite moody and restless, and kept almost entirely to
his own room. We had no doubt that he had received
a rude shock that night; and the effects, instead of
passing away rapidly, seemed to deepen and increase
as each day rolled by. He seemed now to take no
interest in the college, or in the success of our examinations; and, to our great surprise, Coulette, we noticed,
was often closeted with him, and came away sometimes
jubilant, sometimes buried in unpleasant thoughts.
Coulette invited no interchange of confidence at any
time, and we did not offer it. But we made wild conjectures as to these secret conclaves, and surmised
something wrong or unpleasant. Then the report
began to spread—in whispers at first, then more loudly,
then without any concealment—that this was the last
session at Mayfield, and that the old college, to which
many pleasant and not dishonourable memories still
clung, was to be closed up and put into the market.
These things were disquieting enough, and made us
forgetful of all the sweet and beautiful things that
Nature was saying to us and showing us in these long,
warm days, and the lustre and fragrance of the summer
nights. It was amusing, yet a little annoying, to find
Cal all the time pursuing, in amateur detective fashion,
the mystery that hung around the Grinder; and one
could not help feeling that there was some unkindness
in tracing the devious ways and dark, unspoken history
of a man around whose footsteps Time and Fate were
weaving a strong web of downfall and disaster. I don't
know whether the Grinder suspected that we were
plotting to discover his secrets, but his manner was
undoubtedly changed towards Charlie and myself. The
old *brusquerie* and hauteur had disappeared, and the
indications of a broken spirit showed themselves in the
soft, almost servile, way in which he now approached
us.

In one of the long walks which, even during these

warm days of May and early June, Herr Messing and
I were wont to take, chattering away in German and
French alternately, as we struck upon the strand from
the high-road, and looked upon the level, broad reaches
of sand that stretched away to the south, we caught a
glimpse of two figures, not quite so far away as to be
unrecognisable, and there was something in the gait
and shuffle of one that seemed quite familiar to me.

"Do you recognise the figure of that man?" I said to
Herr Messing.

He was rather shortsighted, and answered without
hesitation, "No!"

"I think you know him," I said.

He was interested at once; for he knew so few, that
it would be a pleasure to meet any acquaintance.

"Berhaps zo," he replied, studiously gazing at the
figures before us.

We walked rapidly, and soon overtook them. The
young girl looked quickly over her shoulder, but did
not recognise us; and as I stepped up briskly, and, slap-
ping him on the back, cried out, "Ferris, dear old
fellow, how are you?" a look of recognition came
into her sad eyes, and she held out her hand, and said,
"Alfred is not likely to forget you!"

"Bless me soul! Mr. Austin, how are you? Herr
Messing, is it you? I'm so glad, donche know, to see
you! Bless me soul! This is a surprise!"

The poor fellow looked a little worn, and, with that
sad reminder of faded gentility which shows itself in a
broken glove, or in sleeves white at the seams, he
struck me as one who was going under in the battle of
life. The sister was better dressed, and had an indefinable air of gentility about her, which was markedly
absent from her brother. I walked with the poor tutor,
and managed to leave Herr Messing in charge of Miss
Bellamy.

"How are you getting on?" I said, seeing that he
was growing nervous. "At the old work still—trisect-
ing angles, and working out the theory of probabilities?"

" Well, you know, Mr. Austin," he said, " I can't do
without my diagrams. They are my chief pleasure in
life. But, donche know, I have to come down to
simpler things now to get bread ! "

" What are you doing, then ? " I replied. " Are you
in Trinity, or in the College of Science ? "

He laughed.

" I'm engaged in teaching simple multiplication to
three little boys in Sandymount," he replied; " and part
of my evenings are spent in trying to drill decimals
into a very—very—stupid boy in Rathmines."

" Four pupils ? " I cried.

" Yes," he said; " but you know my sister teaches
music and drawing, and brings in a few shillings. I
w - wish I could free her from such drudgery: she is
deserving of better things. She is as near perfection,
Mr. Austin, as any mortal can be."

He paused, and I saw he was affected. But he shook
it off. Those who have to calculate shillings and pence
cannot afford the luxury of fine feelings.

" But how are you getting on ? " he asked; " and how
is Hugh—I mean—Mr. Bellamy ? "

" There is no use, Alfred," I said, looking him in the
face, and calling him for the first time by his name;
" there is no use in concealing the fact that he is your
brother. We all know that." He looked pained and
surprised. " But there is a curious mystery about him,
which some of us—not I—are anxious to unravel."

" Oh, don't ! " he cried piteously. " Let hidden things
remain hidden. You never know what you may discover. Besides, it is not honourable."

" He has treated you shamefully," I said.

" It makes no matter," he replied. " If he has done
wrong, he has suffered. Leave him in peace."

" But tell me," I queried, " as I am already so indeli-
cate, I may continue—are you ever embarrassed? To
put it plainly, do you ever want money ? "

" No," he said decisively, " I am never in want. We
have no luxuries, but we don't want necessaries. And

some unknown friend sends us money every week. God bless him or her!"

"You don't know the person?" I said, again very churlishly.

"I suspect: I don't know!"

"You suspect whom?"

He blushed and remained silent. I pressed him: he was more embarrassed.

"You or the—the Count!" he said, with a stammer.

Then I felt the most infinitely mean of mortals. I had probed too far, and discovered that the light-hearted, frivolous Count, whom sometimes I despised in my heart, was a hidden hero. But I should confess; and how? I was glad beyond measure that his sister was not near.

"Then it is the Count," I blurted. "God bless him!'

"God bless him and you too!" said the poor fellow, as he sent me down deeper in the valley of humilia-tion.

"But what of your examination?" he inquired, after a pause. "It's coming off soon—is it not?"

"Yes," said I, "and I am badly prepared. Since you left, I have done nothing in mathematics."

"I am very sorry," he replied; "the mathematics will be, you know, the crucial test. Your success depends upon your knowledge of them, donche know?"

"Then," said I, "my chances are small. I have been completely neglecting them for the Classics."

"It's not too late yet," he said. "If—if—I may venture—but no—'twouldn't do! But keep close to your trigonometry, and mind the logarithms."

"Well, no matter," I cried, assuming a cheerfulness I did not quite feel. "I am glad beyond measure to have seen you; and I hope we shall often see you again."

We turned round, and found Herr Messing in an animated conversation with Elsie. The professor was quite excited, and beaming all over with pleasure. Our interruption was not quite welcome.

"Vhy did you goom back?" he cried impatiently; "vhe were joost talking about Jean Paul. Mees Bellamy knows all about him. The only one in Ireland who knows Jean Paul."

"Come now, come now, professor," I said, "this is too bad. Be just to your pupils! You are bewildered, and your memory is gone."

"Ah—ah—mein vrendt," he said, pointing his finger at me, "I do not vorget. You know Jean Paul—his body; but she knows Jean Paul—his soul."

"Come now, explain yourself," I said, with a show of anger.

"Egsplain myself!" said the professor, chagrined. "You English, or Ireesh, cannot understand a *mot*. You want a book. It takes an hour to tell you what, if put in a word, we understandt. Now, Mees Bellamy, you egsplain!"

"I presume," said Elsie, smiling and with a slight blush, "the professor means that men understand merely the language and diction of Richter: women only can understand his spiritual suggestions."

"Now, perhaps you understandt, you blockhead; now you—you—Evans! do you grasp my meaning?"

"Now, professor," I replied, "I make all allowance. You are intoxicated. You are quite out of your senses. Come along, or I don't know what will happen."

With some difficulty he tore himself away, and we bade good-bye to this lonely pair, the last words of the tutor being, "Mind the logarithms, Mr. Austin!" and the last words of the professor, "Vhee vhill talk of Richter again, Mees Bellamy. Read up the 'Titan.'"

"Dot iz an admirable vhoman," said the professor, waking out of a fit of abstraction, as we walked homewards. "I'm beginning to dink better of you all here in Ireland."

"Complimentary, I'm sure!" I replied.

"You zee," he continued, "it takes time to know you here. Now, who would haf thought that an Irish girl had read Richter? And knew Richter well? And had caught Richter's spirit ? I am zure it is a rare bleasure."

" Well, for your sake, Herr Messing," I replied, " I'm glad "—

" And for your zake too," he replied ; " vhee vhill go dere togeder."

" Go where ? " I cried, in astonishment.

" Vhee are going to take tea with dem to-night," he said.

" You don't mean to say you made such an engagement ? " I replied.

"Enzgagement ! dat is one of your queer vords. Enzgagement—a battle ; enzgagement—a contract for marriage ; enzgagement—I am puzzled ! "

This was embarrassing. Yet what could we do ? The delightful simplicity of Herr Messing had led him to contravene all laws, social and collegiate. Or perhaps I should rather say, his German training and honest and rugged nature overleaped the bounds set up by an artificial and most unhealthy condition of society.

We were thinking of such things when, entering the grounds of Mayfield, we came straight upon the Grinder. He was walking up and down, his hands fastened behind him, like a Napoleon, and hardly recognised us until we came quite close to him. Then, altogether disregarding Herr Messing, he linked his arm in mine and forced me to walk with him.

" I'm anxious about your examination," he said abruptly, when the professor was out of hearing. " Our friend and his teaching is all right. You will get best marks in French and German. But what about your mathematics ? "

The very question his brother asked me on the sands an hour ago.

" They are weak enough, sir," I said. " I was getting on fairly well with Mr. Bel— Mr. Ferris," I pulled up like an engine-driver who sees an obstruction before him. The Grinder winced.

11

"But why cannot you get on with this present tutor?"

"I hardly know," I replied, not willing to tell the whole truth; "but he doesn't make the science attractive."

"There's the evil," said the Grinder, vexed. "If he makes it attractive, like your Latin teacher, you lose your senses over it, and become absorbed in it to the exclusion of everything else; if he doesn't make it attractive, you leave him there. Yet he would make you pass your examination."

"You told me," said I, "months ago, that I had no chance!"

"Yes!" said he between his teeth, "because I knew your disposition. I knew right well that you could not settle down to the dull, prosaic work of grinding for an examination. You will fail, and then "—

He stopped.

"And then, sir?" said I.

"And then," said he slowly, "you will eat out your heart in fretting for lost opportunities. The most doleful cry of humanity," he spoke with feeling for which I never gave him credit, "is the cry, 'I might have done better, but now, too late'; or, as some poet phrases it—

> 'Of all sad words of tongue or pen,
> The saddest is this: It might have been.'

It is easy enough for the hot blood and the quick pulses of youth to despise the future, and the consequences of present acts; but, believe me, the most bitter pain of life is to think that we have just missed a golden prize, when by a single effort we might have gained it. Of course there is little use in talking. Experience alone is the world's teacher. But he is a desperate schoolmaster. What he teaches is written in tears and blood."

He seemed to be giving a bit of his own autobiography, for he spoke as one who had suffered.

"Now, Austin, you may suppose it makes no difference to you whether you succeed in this examination or are defeated. You may say to yourself: Well, there are other chances; and I am young and sanguine. No! this is your last chance, I tell you. The department for which you are striving closes its doors this year to all competition for the future, except within the ranks of the army. And I may also tell you, that Mayfield closes its gates this year!"

" What ? " said I, quite off my guard.

" So it is," he said. " I had hopes to make this place a decent academy—the only decent educational establishment in Ireland. You see, I have spared no expense in securing the very best teachers in every department. But it is fate—that awful fate that is pursuing me through life, and will dog my footsteps to the end."

He spoke so sadly that once again my heart went out to him; and I began to believe in that mysterious thing called destiny, and to give up my favourite theory, that man is the architect of his own fortunes.

But he was more softened and humbled than I thought. For, after a pause, he said, with some slight nervousness—

" It is possible, Austin, tnat long since I have forfeited your good opinion. But when you are older and wiser, perhaps you will understand that circumstances have made me what I am. Some day you will learn my story. I admit all appearances are against me. I have not acted well towards the respectable boys here. I did not realise it until you chastised that infamous scoundrel O'Dell; and not even then, until he took his dastardly revenge on Travers. It has been the weakness of my life to lean towards evil-disposed people and to dislike the well-ordered minds of those who keep their passions under submission. Why this is so, God only knows; for He has fearfully punished me. But, when all is revealed, don't think too badly of me. Circumstances have been always against me."

He held out his hand to me for the first time. I grasped it warmly. He strode along towards the house. I could have cried for him.

CHAPTER XX

THE LONELY SCHOLAR

"Peaceful by birthright as a virgin lake,
The lily's anchorage, which no eyes behold
Save those of stars, yet for thy brother's sake
That lay in bonds, thou blew'st a blast as bold
As that wherewith the heart of Roland brake,
Far heard through Pyrenean valleys old."
LOWELL.

WE sat in the little, musty, cigar-scented room which I had not seen since Christmas Eve. The embarrassment of Alfred Bellamy had passed away. Herr Messing, glowing with excitement, was talking some extraordinary jargon to Miss Bellamy, in which I could distinguish only Richter, Siebenkäs, the divine, le poëme de ciel, la langue des anges, etc., etc. We left them to their dreams over against the piano, on whose keys Elsie's fingers went straying as she spoke or listened to the enraptured professor. Alfred and I smoked in silence, the best companionship of men, and looked out at the growing twilight. A poor, stubby escalonia was budding outside the window, and near by, in some sheltered nook, a thrush was singing vespers.

"A curious life yours, Alfred," I said.

"A quiet, happy life, Mr. Austin."

"Uneventful, unemotional, unbroken by vicissitude, and unvaried by new experiences."

"And all the more happy because of those very things."

"But don't you ever dream of doing better?" I inquired.

"I couldn't do better," he said. "Listen." The nervous hesitation had completely disappeared. He was at his ease; and he spoke like a scholar and a gentleman.

"When I rise in the morning, I take a simple break-

fast, and after breakfast I depart for my work—a few
tuitions. It is drudgery, teaching rudiments to stupid
boys—going over the same dry details day by day. I
shouldn't mind teaching clever boys. You remember
how pleasant it was at Mayfield, going over' the deep
mysteries of science. But when my energies flag, I
say, 'Now, Alfred, you cannot afford to dream for four
or five hours to-night, unless you drudge two or three
hours in the morning.' This stimulates me, and I go
through my work. At noon I return. After dinner,
Elsie goes out to her tuitions—she teaches French,
German, and music—a task I would willingly spare
her, but she insists. Sometimes she comes back worn
and tired enough. Girls are more trying than boys ;
and, well, you have no idea what it is to deal with our
nouveaux riches. Imagine a girl like Elsie: you can see
for yourself." I looked, and saw her pale profile, crowned
with masses of auburn hair. She was looking straight
at Herr Messing, who, nothing abashed, continued gesticulating and lecturing as if to a class of boys. She was
olive pale; but there was a look of sweetness and dignity
about her, which only one school of Italian artists gave
the Divine Mother. "Imagine a girl like her, with all
her refinement and real downright actual knowledge of
languages, obliged day after day to listen to the vapid
conceits of some poor lady, who has just reached the
acme of fortune, but has neither knowledge nor humility
enough to bear it well. Sometimes Elsie tells me her
little comedies in the evening, when we are alone ; and
although she has infinite pity for these poor people, I
see it is a strain upon her patience and sweetness."

I thought, what would Madame la Grande, Berkeley
Square, or Mademoiselle Parvenue think, if they heard
the poor drudge, whom they hire at half a guinea a
week, pitying them and dubbing them "poor people."

"But at night," continued Alfred Bellamy, smoking
calmly, and as if he enjoyed the recollection of these
symposia, "at night, when tea is over, and Elsie goes
into the kitchen to see after household matters, I keep

one beloved cup of tea near my desk, light my cigar
and enter the Elysian fields. All the wonders of science
open up before me, and I walk through vistas of en-
chantment, and my magicians open up ever new and
surprising wonders to my enraptured sight. Sometimes
I am out amongst the stars, weighing Algol and its
black satellite, or careering through space as I watch
and calculate the speed of the Groombridge. Then I
suddenly swoop to earth and watch the curiosities of the
microscope, thus connecting the infinitely great and the
infinitely little. Then I lose myself for hours together
at some knotty problem or exercise which suspends all
my faculties like morphia, until I lose all self-conscious-
ness, and have to ask myself when I awake where I am.
At twelve o'clock or so, Elsie comes in and wakes me
up, and then soothes my nerves with a slight, gentle
touch on the piano ; and so *da capo* every day, until,
were it not for Elsie, and my desire to see her better
placed, I think I should regret an invitation even to
heaven, but that we are told that we shall go on there
for ever increasing our knowledge of things, and for ever
growing in our knowledge and love of Him who is the
Maker and Framer of it all."

I was profoundly impressed by his piety and sin-
cerity. What was this passionate thirst after knowledge which was so characteristic of all my professors,
and which made them despise all the ordinary advantages and attractions of life, to exult in the unlimited
acquisition of ideas and sensations? Already, this
example had told on me to my own detriment, as the
Grinder had declared. Would my feelings go on
increasing day by day, until I too should become a
lonely scholar, without ambition, without prospect in
life, save what I saw around me—and no sister to share
my thoughts, and help me with community, not only of
feeling, but of interests? I looked around the poorly-
furnished room. A well-worn carpet; a centre table,
laden with books and mathematical instruments; the
piano, which Elsie's fingers clasped; a few poor prints

on the walls; and the high desk, from which the enraptured student ascended nightly into his heaven;—
would I be content with all this? Then what about
my Oriental dreams, my £600 a year, my gold lace and
epaulettes, and all the fairy scenes Charlie and I were
so fond of conjuring up under the limes these summer
nights? I abruptly changed the subject.

"You are aware," I said, "I suppose, that Mayfield
is to be closed after this session?"

He was quite startled, and his old manner came back
for a moment.

"You don't—don't—s-say so?" he cried. "I—I—
hadn't heard. Why?"

"I don't know," I replied. "Mr. Bellamy is my
authority. It appears things are going against him."

"Poor Hugh! poor Hugh!" he said, in a reverie.
"Everything goes against him. He has been singularly unfortunate."

"And not criminal?" I said. It was thoughtless;
but he flashed up.

"No! no! certainly not. Impulsive, I grant you, and
hasty; but criminal—oh no!"

"I cannot make him out," said I. "He has been so
unjust and unkind, and then again so candid and
friendly, that I am puzzled. Yet I admit, there is some
singular attraction about him that wins you in spite of
your dislikes."

Alfred was uneasy, and shifted in his seat. He
looked at me several times as if he was about to ask,
"Shall I tell you, or shall I not?" The professor was
tired at last, or was it his listener? for he was silent;
and her fingers, straying listlessly over the keys, were
now translating from them some strange dreamy harmony, that filled the room as if with spirits who would
be glad to break the silence and speak once more with
men. I do not know how to call this delicious harmony—whether it is a fugue, or a sonata—and probably
I shall never know; but it passed through every nerve
and fibre like a powerful drug, and left me steeped in

sensations so thrilling and deep that no language could
translate them.   There was a pause after every note,
and an echo like the humming of a deep-mouthed bell;
and if every note was separate and independent, it was
also blended into a mysterious melody, that was infinitely pathetic and touching.   I think I have heard
something like it when, awake at night, I listened in
the pauses of the wind to the raindrops dripping from
the eaves; and there was no noise, nor hurry, nor
fortissimos to the end, but the whole sweetness died
away quietly into silence, and left us staring at one
another and thinking.   The professor was crying like a
child.   I wonder do women ever dream how sublime
they can be, when, with faces lifted to heaven, they
speak to us through the divine medium of music.

Alfred Bellamy continued to smoke in silence, until
we rose to depart.   Once more I feel I was rude and
impertinent, for I said—

"Mr. Bellamy keeps to his room nearly altogether
now.   He sees no one there but Coulette, who is with
him every day."

"But, Coulette, does—does *he* know?"

"Know what, or whom?"

"I was forgetting.   It makes no matter.   Think
kindly of Hugh, if you can, Mr. Austin!"

As we returned home in the warm night, the
professor was beside himself in enthusiasm and indignation.

"Remember, it is I, it is not you, who have discovered her!"

"What ails you, professor?   Discovered whom?"

"Id takes us Germans to disgover you Irish.   Our
scholars know your language and disgover your literature.   Our exiles disgover your geniuses.   You are
purblind.   You zee noding but your green rag, you
hear noding but 'Patrick's Day in the Morning.'   You
know noding of yourselves but what we do tell you."

I waited.

"Dere now is that young, bright genius.   You did

not know her: her broder does not know her: no one
knows her. And yet she is a genius, mein Gott! how
great! If she were in Weimar, men would flock around
her and adore her. If Wagner could zee her, he would
make her his immortal pupil. But here she is; and
here she vhill remain—a vlower amongst weeds, a
pearl before swine!"

"You are becoming complimentary, Herr Messing,"
I said; "but then you are always so."

"How can I help it?' he cried vehemently. "You
are a nation of geniuses, zurrounded by anoder nation of
blockheads; and the blockheads are the masters."

Then he fell into a reverie, muttering snatches from
Goethe and Schiller, and keeping up an imaginary conversation with Miss Bellamy, until we reached the
gates and entered. I saw in the twilight under the
trees the gaunt form of the Grinder swinging to and fro
in a rapid walk, his gown gathered up, and his hands
clasping his square cap behind his back. He didn't
seem to notice us, and we passed silently into the college.
But up to eleven o'clock, in the intervals of my reading,
I could see the black figure under the trees, now paus-
ing as if arguing with an unseen antagonist, now striding
on rapidly again. The bats were circling round about
the strange figure, but he did not heed them; and the
three sisters were weaving around him a close, clinging
web; but if he ever dreamt of their presence, it was, I
am sure, to shake off the gloomy presentiments that
foreshadowed their work, and to whisper to himself lines
he was rather fond of—

"I have no fears for the vengeful years,
But I lift up my face to defy them all."

CHAPTER XXI

A LETTER

" But to be wroth with those we love
Doth work like madness in the brain."
                                        COLERIDGE.

THE growth of two failings—one physical, the other
intellectual—at this time was so gradual and insensible,
that it is only now, after the lapse of many years, that I
have become fully conscious of it. The mental strain
of hard, protracted study had produced a curious
nervous irritability, that exhibited itself in a peevish-
ness that was really foreign to my character; and I
had begun to assume a certain conceit or priggishness
of manner, at whose absurd manifestations I can now
afford to smile. I do not know whether it was my
acquaintance with the lords of human learning, or the
superciliousness of a youth who had not yet tasted the
bitterness of life, that created the ridiculous assumption
of a superiority that had no more solid basis than half
the pretensions of the young. But, unquestionably, I
had become disagreeable to myself and to others; and,
as usual in such cases, I placed the fault at the door of
everyone else, and completely exculpated myself. This
was particularly noticeable in my relations with Charlie
Travers. No two friends were ever brought together
more closely, or by so many happy ties; yet the "little
rift within the lute" had unquestionably begun to
widen. His transcendental ideas were quite beyond my
comprehension; and I, a dreamer, an enthusiast, had no
sympathy whatever with the grand spiritual idealism
which, I could see, was gradually absorbing his whole
being. And as, during our brief sojourn at his father's
house, I resented, and was irritated by, the very exalted
teaching and example of Father Aidan, so at present I
resented anything approaching a contradiction of the

principles that now animated me. But Charlie's whole life, manner, principles, habits, were thus in contradiction, and therefore a constant and tacit reproach. His health, only partly rehabilitated by the run to Clare, began again to show signs of feebleness; and I noticed, from time to time, something that seemed in him unnatural excitement. His eyes would brighten, and he would talk in a strain quite sanguine and hopeful, and then lapse into unusual depression again. I found that he was using a drug, recommended by some country doctor as a safe stimulant. It was some kind of bromide, and was advertised as an innoxious and effective help in cases where there was much mental languor and exhaustion. I had sense enough to know that the use of drugs of any kind at such a time could not but be harmful; and I remonstrated with Charlie. He laughed it off, and urged me to take to the same habit. I pressed him. He became serious; then he said pathetically—

"You don't know, Goff, what I suffer sometimes. Between the strain of constant study—the wish to succeed, to please mother—the desire that I may fail, in order that I may turn to something more in accordance with my better wishes—the dread of the future, the horror of the present—I am utterly miserable. Suspense and uncertainty are the hardest things to be borne in life."

"But, my dear fellow," I said, with a hopefulness I was far from feeling, "you and I must only do our best, and leave our futures in the hands of — of" — I was going to say God, but the word stuck in my throat—"of Fate."

He looked at me sadly.

"We are drifting, Goff," he said at last; "and God only knows whitherward!"

Then for the first time I felt that the penalty of culture—education, whatever else you call it—is isolation. The gods take you up into a high mountain apart, and you must break every human tie that binds you to your friends who labour in the valleys.

It was another lesson in such bitterness, when, a few days later, to my surprise, a letter from my guardian, from whom I had not heard for six months, was put into my hands. It ran thus:—

" MY DEAR GOFF,—I write, after a long silence, to say that unhappily my last letter was a direct injustice to you, and was written perhaps too hastily, under information which, I have now reason to believe, was untrue. If in that letter there was any expression that might have pained you, I beg that you will forget it. Perhaps, indeed, you have reason to feel aggrieved that I should have in so short a time thrown doubts upon your honourable instincts, and those principles of religion which I know are so dear to you. I admit, after your solemn asseverations, and, above all, the sacred promise you made me on your deceased mother's grave, it was quite wrong to throw doubt upon your fidelity to such grave promises. I wish now to say that I have perfect confidence in you; and I hope you will confide in me. From what I have lately heard from your superiors, I am quite happy to believe that you are in your studies a credit to your college, and in your habits of life, your steadfastness to principle, and your fidelity to the practices of religion, quite a model and example to the other students. Let me know how you are. I send you a small remittance, and shall be happy to send you more money on hearing from you.—I am, my dear Goff, yours always affectionately,

                              " T. COSTELLOE."

It is doubtful whether the former letter stung me so deeply as this. The coals of fire, slung from all quarters, were heaping themselves steadily on my head. What had I done? I had had quite an honourable record, and behold! on every side voices were calling to me, upbraiding, chiding under praise, arguing against all my new instincts, tormenting me with doubts and self-questionings, when all I wanted was to be let severely

alone. I resented it deeply. I lifted my head against
God, Fate, and the messengers that were sent me. I
stiffened my neck, and hardened my heart, and steeled
my nerves, and said, deep down in my soul, " Quare
conturbas ? " and deeper still, heard only by accusing
spirits that flung it at me in later life for my punishment and remorse, " Non serviam ! "

I took that letter, tore it into minutest fragments
leisurely and deliberately, and flung it to the four winds
of heaven.

That evening I had a succession of visitors. First
came the Grinder.

" Your papers have come, Austin. You go to London
for examination this day week."

" How long will it last ? "

" Between preliminaries and the ora] and written, the
better part of three weeks."

I groaned.

" I would advise you to let all reading alone for
this week. What you can do these few days is but
little ; and it will be a matter of supreme importance
for you to face your examiners with an unclouded
mind."

" And what am I to do for this week ? "

" Absolutely nothing."

" That will be the hardest part of my work."

" You must face it. I'll tell Travers the same. He
needs rest more than you."

A sudden impulse seized me.

" I am sorry you are not coming with us, sir," I said.
He smiled.

" Do you imagine I could be of any use to you ? "

" The greatest."

" Well, it's kind of you to say it, Austin," he said.
" But it's impossible. And remember, lad," he said,
rising, " you stand or fall by yourself in this world.
Men are but feeble props at best."

" I'm thinking," I said, " what I shall do if I'm
spun."

"Of course you'll go straight to your guardian."

"Quite out of the question," I replied.

"Ah, my boy," said he, laying his hand affectionately on my shoulder, "you'll change those opinions yet. You'll learn, after many trials, that the best thing in this world is the friendship of a good man."

An hour later, the Count came in. We were great friends since he expelled O'Dell. He said abruptly, sitting on the arm of my study chair—

"I don't like too well what your friend Charles comes from doing."

"What do you refer to, Henri?"

"I think he indulges too much in what you call stimulants."

"I hope not," I said; "I believe it is only some medicine, or tonic, the doctor has given him."

"Perhaps so," he replied; "but I should be sorry. I rather like him. He will accomplish something great yet, if he has the chance. He is all nerve: an enthusiast, a dreamer. I can see the shadows of future conquests in his eyes."

"He is everything you say, Henri. I am delighted that you appreciate him."

"All the more reason for preventing a wreck. And wrecked he will be if he perseveres in using these dangerous drugs."

After a few moments, he resumed—

"I shall be sorry to leave here. Not that it was all that I expected, or was taught to expect, but one meets with spirits that one would be loth to part with for ever."

"I am sure," I said, "we shall all miss your courage and courtesy."

Then, in a bantering tone—

"If I am spun at the examination, I shall enlist as a French hussar."

He smiled, and then, fearing there was irony in my words, he said—

"It was once an honour to serve under the tricolor."

"I should esteem it an honour still."'

"Well, we are disgraced, of course. But a Napoleon will arise yet, and retrieve our honour. Your countrymen were once glad enough to serve under the French flag."

"Don't mistake me, Henri," I said. "I am not inclined to depreciate either the bravery or honour of France. If I had no other attraction, I should be glad to be with you."

He looked me steadily between the eyes, and, feeling satisfied that I was not sarcastic, he said, "Thank you," and withdrew.

Now, this was not quite calculated to compose my nerves, so, when Cal burst in later in the evening, and shouted—

"I have found out all, Goff. The veil is lifted. Hurrah!" I could not help saying—

"What do you mean now, you miserable little spy?"

The poor little fellow, usually so audacious and cool, shrank into himself, and said, in a whisper—

"What have I done?"

"What have you done?" I cried, quite irritated; "you have been peering and spying into the private life of a man whose life is beyond suspicion. You have been dogging his footsteps, and ransacking every detail of his history. And for what? Simply to satisfy an insane curiosity. The whole thing is disgraceful and dishonourable in the extreme."

Cal had by this time recovered his equanimity, and, rolling a cigarette between his fingers, he sat on the edge of my bed, studiously silent.

I went on with my logarithms, but my brain would not work. The long, hateful columns swam before my eyes. I could not concentrate my thoughts for an instant, and the old refrain of Mr. Dowling, "What is your d——d A plus B to that?" went ringing through my ears. I flung the arithmetic aside impatiently, and took up Cicero. I turned over page after page in haste, and found nothing to my taste. I tried a line or two. In vain. My thoughts flew off at a tangent, as you would fling water from a brush. And at last, overcome by my irritability, I flung aside all books, and shouted to Cal—

"Well, what is it, you d——d little beggar?"

CHAPTER XXII

THE VEIL UPLIFTS

τοὺς μὲν καθαρὰς
χεῖρας προνέμοντας
Οὗτις ἀφ' ἡμῶν μῆνις ἐφέρπει,
'Ασινὴς δ' αἰῶνα διοιχνεῖ·
Οστις δ' ἀλιτρῶν, ὥσπερ ὅδ' ἀνὴρ
χεῖρας φονίας ἐπικρύπτει,
Μάρτυρες ὀρθαὶ τοῖσι θανοῦσιν
Παραγιγνόμεναι, πράκτορες αἵματος
Αὐτῷ τελέως ἐφάνημεν.

"On him, indeed, who possesses pure hands, no wrath from us steals, but, free from harm, he passes into life; but whosoever, committing crime like this man, conceals his stained hands, close at hand, like true witnesses to the deed, we appear with might as avengers of blood to him."

ÆSCHYLUS, *Eumenides*, 313-321.

"GOFF," said Cal calmly, "you are an interesting pathological subject. Physically, you are an excellent specimen of humanity; but from the psychical point of view, I fear you are a 'degenerate.' Your nervous system is not only unstrung, but shattered. I am not quite sure, until I make a more careful diagnosis, whether it is the sensory or vaso-motor nerves that are affected; but, undoubtedly, the cortex of the grey cerebral tissue, the seat of thought "—

I suppose he saw my hand moving suspiciously to a heavy Lemprière, for he made a beseeching gesture.

"Go on with your story, you young imp," I cried; "not that I want to hear it "—he smiled—"but anything will do just now to take me from myself."

"I was just about to say," said Cal, "that the most alarming sign of your nervous degeneracy is that your memory is failing. Who first suggested a mystery in connection with Hugh Bellamy? Who put me on his track? Who stimulated me by praise? Who urged me when I lagged? Who offered the highest reward in his power, his own unappreciable esteem, to the detective who would ferret out this dark history? Ah, I see—'Conscience doth make cowards of us all'!"

"I am honestly ashamed of whatever part I have taken in this disreputable matter," I said.

"Well, perhaps so," said Cal. "Now, listen for some higher motive (as a salve to your tender conscience) than mere curiosity.

"Sometime back in the fifties, two figures might be seen emerging from the fast express that reached San Francisco at four o'clock in the afternoon of a warm summer day. That is Henry James's style. One was an old ecclesiastic; the other a young athlete, with dark curls Apollonian, and a slight stoop on his shoulders, à la *Thersites*. Do you recognise the pictures?"

"Yes," I said; "go on."

"They did not tarry in 'Frisco, as our good sailors call it, but went straight thence to Santa Barbara, an old Franciscan mission on the Pacific coast. This was out of their way; for the object of the aged ecclesiastic, whom your quick apprehension has recognised as Father Bellamy, was to collect funds for the Catholic University of Dublin. But the young man, whom your inner consciousness recognises as Hugh Bellamy, *alias* the Grinder, hurried him on, on a quick tour of observation around the Pacific coast. They remained at Santa Barbara."

I sat up. I was interested.

"I see, your curiosity—no, your higher sense—is at last aroused. Well, patience has its reward. You were going to ask why they tarried at Santa Barbara. Well, there was in that mediæval town an ancient church, dedicated to St. James of Compostella. In charge of the church was an old Franciscan—mediæval, brown, shaggy, an ascetic, and a saint. In charge of the old Franciscan was a young ward—not mediæval, brown, not an ascetic, but a saint. To her was introduced Hugh Bellamy, Esq., M.A., a young barrister, in

12

large practice in Dublin, and on the high road to silk
and the ermine—perhaps the Woolsack. Result—matri-
monial advertisement in *San Francisco Chronicle*, that
Hugh Bellamy, Esq., M.A., barrister-at-law, Baggot
Street, Dublin, was married to Doña Isabella Pia
Coléto, on 11th July 18—, at the Church of St. Iago
di Compostella, Santa Barbara."

Cal stopped and looked at me inquiringly.

"Do you follow me?"

"Yes!"

"You see no reason for surprise?"

"No!"

"Blessed stupidity! Well, to proceed. In September of the same year, Father Bellamy and Hugh
left the Pacific coast for Ireland. The business of the
former was finished, that is, a finished failure. The
latter bade farewell to his young bride, having previously obtained a deed, signed by her, and which
handed over to him all her estates, in cotton and
tobacco, valued at £20,000. He never saw his bride
again. Did he care? I don't know. I am narrating
facts; I am not analysing sensations. In October, he
was in Dublin. He had only come back, of course, to
prepare a house, etc., for his wife. He at once leaped
into a considerable practice. He figured chiefly as a
chamber lawyer. His opinion on intricate questions
was never controverted. Leading men at the Bar,
judges even, sent their sons to be coached by him for
examination. In the delirium of success that winter
he forgot Santa Barbara and the Doña Isabella,
although, of course, in constant correspondence. He
formed a new engagement. His marriage was a profound secret. Ambition and the desire for advancement
blinded him, and hardened his conscience. He was
married at the Pro-Cathedral, Marlborough Street,
Dublin, in July 18—. You are horrified?"

"I am."

"It was not quite so bad as it appears. But the
guilt was his all the same. The lady whom he hon-

oured a second time was the daughter of Frederick
Houston, then president of one of our highest colleges.
Her name was Marcella."

I jumped up.

"The lady in the asylum?"

"The same! A few weeks after her marriage, it
transpired that he had been married before. Apparently he was guilty of bigamy. Really he was not.
Doña Isabella Pia Coléto had died the May previous.
The consequences to him were, however, the same. He
was ostracised and disbarred, and saved from prosecu-
tion and penal servitude only by the difficulty of getting evidence from such a distant quarter as Santa
Barbara. His second wife lost her reason."

Cal paused, as if he had piled up agony enough. I
was silent, as this strange story of crime or madness
knocked to pieces my own theories about the Grinder,
built, I must say, chiefly on his own statements, and
the pathetic appeal his brother made for him. Not
that my sympathy with the unhappy man, now clearly
consumptive, and with the handwriting of death upon
his face, was in the smallest degree diminished. Nay,
I felt for him more than ever, as I perceived how fate
and his own passions had conspired to weave for him
that Nessus-shirt of torture and shame. But how could
I excuse him? What apology could be offered for
such criminality?

"Have you any more to tell?" I asked.

"Yes," said Cal emphatically. Then, after a pause,
he said, with great deliberation—

"Do you remember my telling you, on the evening
when your Serene Highness arrived here, that there
was but one boy in the house whom the Grinder feared,
and whom he would not punish?"

"I think I do. You mean Coulette?"

"I do. Do you remember why I made that remark?"

"I remember there was some scene between himself
and the Grinder."

"Precisely. Can you put two and two together?"

I looked at Cal bewildered.

"You see nothing?"

"No!"

"Œdipus was a telescope to you! Do you mean to say you suspect nothing?"

"Absolutely nothing! You are mystifying me."

"Well, I'll lead you by degrees. Meat for men, milk for children. Let me see. Do you remember the name I gave you as that of the Grinder's first wife?"

"Yes. Doña Isabella Pia Coléto."

"You see nothing still?"

"Absolutely nothing."

"Kindly pronounce the last word again."

"Coléto," I said, bewildered.

"How would you put it in French?"

"Coulette."

The whole thing flashed on my stupid brain, and I jumped from my chair in surprise.

"Soyez tranquille! mon ami. It is so. Coulette is the son of Hugh Bellamy and the Doña Isabella."

I was humbled, shamed, crushed by the cleverness of this little mite. He stood head and shoulders over me. I was a pigmy compared to him. What was all my learning compared with this natural astuteness, that could track like a Red Indian? I humbly apologised.

"I retract every word I said, Cal. I am a fool."

Then, after a pause of utter bewilderment, I ventured to ask this master—

"Does the Grinder know it?"

I·was afraid of a repulse; but Cal had had his victory, and was satisfied.

"No—that is, not yet. He'll know it soon."

"Does Coulette know it?"

In presence of this detective genius, I hesitated to ask the question. Cal replied—

"What do you think brought Coulette here?"

"To be educated, I suppose"

Cal smiled.

"You might as well think of educating a leopard. Not at all. He came here with the fullest knowledge of all that has happened, with his fiery heart scorched and blackened against the man who abandoned his mother, and with the dark determination to recover that deed from the Grinder, even at the cost of life."

"That deed can have been of little use to the Grinder?"

"None whatever. He never drew a penny from the cotton and tobacco plantation. The old Franciscan drew all its revenues, and has them stored up for Coulette."

"But how did Coulette restrain himself all this time?"

"Just as a wild beast who waits to be fed. Do you see that path under the bushes? It is worn white. Have you not seen Coulette trampling out that path for the last nine months, and trampling the Grinder at every step? Did you never notice him swinging his sombrero, and gesticulating like a madman? Henri did—when he was here but a week. I did. The boy is a living volcano, and we are very near the eruption. He has been visiting the Grinder's room lately nearly every day under one pretence or another. In reality, he has been studying the Grinder's weak points, and has been looking out for the place where the deed was possibly concealed."

It is curious how the strength of a new-born interest and affection stifles the weak protests of principle. I had fully made up my mind, whilst Cal was speaking, to put the Grinder on his guard, detestable though his conduct undoubtedly was to these poor victims. But there were a few points I wished to see cleared up.

"What has been the history of his brother and sister?"

"The same story," said Cal, not unwillingly, "of cruelty and desertion and contempt. It appears that the Bellamys were quite a respectable family, which became rapidly reduced in circumstances; that whatever was saved from the wreck and ruin of their fortunes was spent on the education of Hugh; that Alfred and his sister, after their weak mother's death, were driven from poverty to utter destitution; that Alfred had become a monitor in a National School at £6 or £8 a year, and his sister was driven to the profession of a street singer."

I thought he was going to say something more terrible, for I remembered the interview between Alfred and his brother; and I drew a deep sigh of relief.

"To show you the ways of that mysterious agent, called Destiny," said Cal, "in which you are, of course, too advanced a thinker to believe, it would appear that the very first night Hugh Bellamy and Marcella Houston appeared at the opera on their return from Paris, the sister whom you know as Elsie sang under that last gas-lamp, do you remember, facing down to Sackville Street; her brother and his bride came down the steps of the Theatre-Royal, and, just as they were about to enter their carriage, Bellamy was recognised by his sister, who then and there fainted—from hunger and exposure, I suppose. It would appear that Mrs. Bellamy, touched with compassion, appealed to her husband to look after the wretched girl. Elsie was taken to the nearest public-house, warmed, and dosed with brandy. When she awoke to consciousness, the face that she saw bending down over her was that of her brother. There was an immediate recognition. She cried, "Oh, Hugh! I am so sorry!" He muttered an oath, and went back to his carriage and the luxuries he was dearly purchasing. He has never seen his sister since. He consented, at the earnest request of Father Bellamy, to take in here, as tutor, his brother Alfred, but on condition of changing his name. Now you know all."

"Just one moment, Cal! When is the *dénouement* to take place? When is Coulette going to make a scene with the Grinder?"

"At any moment. He knows now that Mayfield

will be closed immediately. He wants but the deed
—and his revenge—and he will quit the country at
once."

"Do you think there will be any violence ? "

"I don't know. It's hard to say. When Greek
meets Greek, or when steel strikes flint, you know the
result."

CHAPTER XXIII

COULETTE DEPARTS

"Be absolute for Death ; either death or life
Shall thereby be the sweeter. Reason thus with life,—
If I do lose thee, I do lose a thing
That none but fools will keep : a breath thou art,
(Servile to all the skyey influences,)
That dost this habitation, where thou keep'st,
Hourly afflict."

Measure for Measure.

THERE was no more study for me that night. I was
tossed between the conflicting sensations of violent
repulsion towards the Grinder, and pity and sympathy
for a poor consumptive, on whom the hand of Death was
already laid. Undoubtedly he was a brute. His was a
career characterised by selfishness, culminating in crime,
and selfishness exhibited towards those, particularly, who
had indisputable claims on his sympathy and protection.
"I wouldn't speak to such a monster. I shall have
nothing more to do with him." But then, my first
encounter with him: his pitiable cry, 'Ah, mother!'
when the infallible death-sign of hæmorrhage showed
itself—his subsequent softening towards myself and
others, which seemed a manifestation of sorrow—and
above all, his position as the victim on whom Death
had already laid his omnipotent hands, changed the
current of my thoughts, and made me resolve to avert,

as far as I could, any further catastrophe that might embitter a heart already charged with compunction, and hasten an end that was speedily approaching.

I thought the matter over that evening, with the result that next day, in an interval of classes, I appeared in the Grinder's room. He was surprised enough, for it was my first voluntary visit. And I was surprised; for the room was not the study of a solitary recluse, but the sumptuous apartment of a leisured and wealthy Sybarite. Books, of course, lined the walls, flashing in all the grandeur of vellum and gold and purple; mirrors duplicated and reduplicated every figure and article of *vertu* in the apartment; handsome clocks ticked, and sang out the bell-notes of the quarters; vases, Oriental, hand-painted, that might have been purloined from a Persian harem, filled every available nook, and covered the inlaid cabinets that hid themselves in every corner; and dainty little paintings gave a colour and a brightness to the dim spaces that stretched from the mouldings of the rich bookcases to the ceiling. The Grinder's back was turned to me as I entered, and I saw that he was using an inhaler, if the strong odour of creosote had not already apprised me of the fact.

" Well, Austin," said he kindly, " what can I do for you ?"

As he turned round, the light shone full on his face. It was haggard and drawn, and his strong teeth showed painfully through the curtains of his lips that were drawn backwards. The silver was very visible in his black hair, especially over the ears and back from the temples. There was a slight moisture of perspiration on his forehead, and he coughed lightly, but not altogether without pain. He had visibly changed in the last few days, and for the worse; and at the sight of this doomed man, all the chill stiffness and dignity I had been summoning up speedily vanished. He motioned me to a chair, and looked curiously at me. I did not know how to begin.

" It is something more than a Greek particle or accent

has brought you, Austin," he said. "What is troubling you?"

"It is nothing concerning myself, sir," I said; "but I thought it a duty to come to you."

"Travers ill again?" he conjectured.

There was no use in prolonging my own agony, so I blurted out—

"No, sir; it is something that concerns yourself intimately."

And there was such a dread in this man's mind of the Parcæ, who were for ever weaving webs for his humiliation and pain, that he grew paler than he was, and gasped out—

"Some other trial, no doubt. Come, we'll face it."

"I am afraid, sir," I continued, "I have been presumptuous"—

"Look here, Austin," he cried; "say anything you like, but let me have no suspense."

Thus conjured, I had no alternative.

"Coulette has been visiting you very much lately, I believe, sir?"

"Yes," he replied; "he came in a few times to ask about some books on the Aztecs."

"He was curious about something else, sir," I replied; "he was looking for a covenant, or deed, made by his mother, and which you hold."

The Grinder looked bewildered for a moment, as if unable to grasp the full meaning of what I had said. Then, looking at me sternly, he said—

"*His* mother? Which *I* hold?"

"Yes, sir," I said, half choking; "Coulette is your son, and he knows it."

"It is a damned lie!" he cried, jumping from his chair in a fit of fury. "How dare you say such a thing?" He fell back exhausted. I was silent.

"You have come here to insult me again, Austin, you take advantage of my helpless condition—you know now how powerless I am." He looked at me in a paroxysm of terror and pain.

"God knows, sir," said I fervently, "it is about the last thing I would think of doing. I came to save you from a scene with Coulette, and from his probable violence."

"But you are labouring under an extraordinary delusion," he said, calming a little. "Coulette is from Sacramento, sent here by a priest whom Father Bellamy met in his travels."

"Perhaps I am mistaken, sir," said I, rising; "but you will pardon me. I thought of nothing but saving you from pain."

"Well, sit down, Austin," he cried; "let us hear the matter out. What have you heard to encourage such a delusion?"

I saw clearly that he half suspected the truth: otherwise he would have dismissed me in anger. But it was a terrible revelation to him.

"I know I am incurring your displeasure, sir," I said, sitting down; "and I had much rather, now that I have put you upon your guard, retire."

"No," said he; "I give you credit for your good intentions: I am always so hasty, and my illness makes me irritable. What you say is inconceivable. But if a blow is to fall on me, at least let me see it. I hate to be struck by an invisible hand."

"Then I may speak freely?" I asked.

"Yes," he replied; "say all that you know, and all that you imagine."

Thus pressed, I told him the whole story of his crimes and their Nemesis, leaving out the details about his brother and sister, and softening and excusing his sin where I could do so conscientiously. He listened with his handkerchief pressed to his eyes, without a sound or a sigh. When I had finished, he said—

"Is that all?"

"That is all that concerns you now, sir," I said.

He went over to the window, and continued gazing long and earnestly at the trees or sky, in the old familiar attitude, with his hands under his light silk gown. The light, hacking cough was subdued under his intense mental excitement. I am quite sure he remained a quarter of an hour in this reverie, for I heard the clocks chiming a quarter and a half hour. Then he heaved a deep sigh; and, as if he had been quite unconscious of my presence, he started on seeing me. I broke the painful silence.

"You know, sir," I said, "if I can be of any use to you in this painful matter, you may command me."

"Do you know, Austin," he said, not heeding my offer, "you have almost reconciled me with Death. For weeks and months that horrible phantom has been creeping towards me. I saw it in my dreams: it was the first thing that made my heart leap and then sink in terror, when I awoke. You know I have never been buoyed up with that strange delusion, that insanity which consumption always brings—the idea that I should recover. No; I have seen Death coming closer and closer every day, sending his red signal before him in this blood," he pointed to a handkerchief, slightly stained, "and sounding his approach in every cough that racked me. And I dreaded him. I did. Reason as I would, Death was a phantom of terror. What you have told me this morning makes of him an angel of mercy. I am a doomed man—doomed not only to death, but to disgrace. Death will be welcome. As Claudio said to the friar—

> "I humbly thank you:
> To sue to live, I find, I seek to die;
> And seeking death, find life: let it come on."

He paused for a moment to cough. Then he resumed—

"I had a hope that I might have finished this little work before I died"—he pointed to a huge pile of manuscript, which I had not noticed—"for it contains all that I had worthy of being said to my fellow-men. But it must not be. My sole regret now is leaving you."

He had walked over to his bookcase, and run his fingers along the leather backs of his books, just as a dying father might run his thin hand through the fair curls of his child. He took down, one by one, his favourite authors, looked at the title-pages, and at some pencilled passages here and there, and replaced them gently and reverently. Then he heaved a deep sigh, and, locking his bookcases, returned to his desk.

"It is hard to leave them. Austin. They were my best friends."

Then, as if musing to himself, he said, after a pause—

"It is dreadful to think of these being scattered through every musty, dusty, second-hand bookstall in the city, to be handled by every idiot, and put back as worthless. I think I should haunt such places, to prevent such a desecration."

"I don't think you need, sir," I said boldly, for I had struck upon quite an original yet audacious idea. "I know those who would prize those glorious books for their own sake, as well as for yours."

"Some students, I suppose?" he said carelessly.

"No," said I; "but your own flesh and blood."

"Ha!" said he, starting up. "You don't mean Coulette?"

"Certainly not!" I replied. "I mean your brother and sister."

The old dark spirit that had hung over him with his wings of fury and despair, seemed to be again taking possession of him. But he was exhausted. Nature was unable to answer the summons of that proud, imperious spirit. He said wearily—

"Leave me now, Austin. Let me think."

I stood up to depart; but the opportunity was too good to let slip.

"Look here, sir," said I, "I'll make a bargain with you. Give me that parchment, and promise me to see your good brother and sister immediately, and I'll guarantee that Coulette will trouble you no more."

He looked undecided. He had forgotten the possi-

bility of an interview with Coulette; and now it began
to assume an aspect of terror to his weak nerves. Yet
the old dominance of pride held him back. How could
he receive those whom he had so grievously injured ?
I moved to the door. If I could reconcile this proud
man to his generous brother and his loving sister, it
would be one good work done in my life at least.
And imagine poor old Ferris with all these gods and
demigods of science and literature smiling down on
him! What glorious nights he would have! What a
symposium with all his heroes!

"I am going to midday class, sir," I said, with my
hand on the glass handle of his study door; "I'll run
over again before dinner."

"No!" he said, with a final effort, "*che sara, sara.*
Here's that document, and do what seems best to you."

I took the yellow parchment, ran upstairs, and locked
it in.

The following afternoon I had a professional visit
from Cal. He looked crestfallen and humbled.

"Well, what's up now ? You look like a Comanche
who has lost tracks."

Cal looked at me dubiously; but as I appeared quite
as irritable as the day before, his suspicions were lulled
asleep.

"It's only a transformation-scene in the pantomime,"
he said. "The villain of the play has absconded, and
there has been a reconciliation all round."

"You look disappointed," I said.

"I'm disgusted," he replied sulkily.

"But explain yourself, if you can," I said. "What
has occurred now ?"

"What has occurred ? The last thing I wanted. I
had been living in anticipation of a scene. Coulette
closeted with the Grinder—angry words—fierce in-
vective—stern demands for justice—recrimination—a
scuffle—a blow—exit Coulette for the Pacific—probably
a paragraph in the *Irish Times*, etc., etc."

"Well ?"

"Just as I tell you. The unexpected always happens. There has been no scene. Coulette has departed; and, *mirabile dictu!* the persons closeted with the Grinder are—you'd never guess?"

"Charlie and the Count?"

"Ridiculous! Old — Ferris — and — his sister!!"

"Look here, Cal, you're joking. The whole thing has been got up by you for a piece of fun. Now, I give you a word of advice. Drop practical joking, and take a serious view of life"—

"Then you don't believe a word of what I am saying?"

"I wouldn't be so impolite as to suggest such a thing. But you would do better at your French or German, than pursuing such subjects, and trying to practise your effete jokes upon me."

Poor Cal! he looked at me once more, in his old inquiring way.

"I think there's an epidemic of insanity broken out somewhere. I wonder am I altogether sane?" he said.

CHAPTER XXIV

BURLINGTON HOUSE

"What is this knowledge! but the sky-stol'n fire
  For which the thief, still chained in ice, doth sit!
And which the poor rude satyr did admire,
  And needs would kiss, but burnt his lips with it!

What is it! but the cloud of empty rain
  Which, when Jove's guest embraced, he monsters got!
Or the false pails which, oft being filled with pain,
  Received the water, but retained it not!

In fine, what is it! but the fiery coach
  Which the youth sought, and sought his death withal!
Or the boy's wings which, when he did approach
  The sun's hot beams, did melt, and let him fall."
                                        SIR JOHN DAVIES.

THE evening before our departure for examination in London, Herr Messing and I paid a visit to Alfred

Bellamy. I had a few questions to ask him on some knotty mathematical problem, which there was one chance in a thousand I might be asked. But one does not like to risk that chance, where so much is at stake. The dear fellow was reading when we entered, and threw into the fireplace the stump of a cigar he was smoking.

"If I succeed, Alfred," said I, "I'll send you the best box of Havanas in London."

He was an inveterate smoker, but was too poor to consume any but the plainest tobacco, except when a friend made him an occasional present. In this matter the Count was infinitely kind. And the first idea one got of Alfred Bellamy's house was that it was a small edition of a hotel coffee-room, or a smokers' club in miniature. This evening he appeared in excellent spirits, was well dressed, and had apparently abandoned for ever that *gaucherie* in speech and manner that made him so obnoxious to his cultured brother. After half an hour or so, his sister came in. I knew where she had been; but she was all the brighter and better for it. Yet there was just a tinge of sorrow in her calm, placid face, as if she thought that one thing only remained to complete their happiness. But this was not to be. She got tea ready; and as I sat straight opposite to her at table, I had full leisure to observe her closely. And my observation now was strengthened by the curious lights and shadows which Cal's discoveries had thrown over her sad history. She appeared to be the most calm, unconscious creature I ever saw. Not a trace of passion or uneasiness or regret or bitterness was visible on her calm, white brow. Neither did a smile break its solemnity and peace. But there was an indefinable peace and serenity that was worth more than ripples of laughter, or those inane attempts at making themselves pleasant, which disfigure and deform so much of what is really beautiful in women. I said, as I watched that immobile face, and thought how it had been lashed with midnight rains in the Dublin streets, and what an awful *inferno* of hideous and revolting images had passed before those calm, clear eyes, that if ever I should need a kindly word or look to keep me from stumbling on the hard road ot life, it would be to some such gentle spiritual being I would have recourse, certain of seeing there something more than human sympathy, and of hearing words that would have the form and colour of inspiration. And who shall say that this young girl would have looked a Sibyl to me, or that my imagination would have woven such a halo of sanctity around her, if she had not passed through the fiery ordeal, and emerged strengthened and purified from that baptism of fire and agony in which all choice souls are cleansed and sanctified and elevated? It is quite possible that, if I had been brought up in the outside world, or in that microcosm of petty ideas and warped and degraded sentiments called society, I might have shared some of that shameful scorn and contempt that made her brother shrink from her as something scorched and blackened. That frightful conventionalism that contemns even pure and holy things, when associated with squalor and poverty, would infallibly have biassed my mind against the young girl. And if I have reason to be grateful for any gift during life, it is that I have never considered the wrappings and bandages with which men and women conceal, and even decorate, their deformities; and that my mind has gone straight to a consideration of character, without the smallest regard for the adventitious circumstances that make so much of the hollow dignities and the insincere professions of men. The same simplicity and straightforwardness characterised most of us at Mayfield, and made me often wonder in after life whether that valuable counsellor called Experience, which is won to our side at such bitter cost, is, after all, worth the chivalry and honour of youth.

"You are treaming, Austin," said the professor, who was trying to eat huge slices of cake and talk poetry simultaneously.

" Well, to-morrow," I said, rousing myself, " would make anyone dream."

Herr Messing had come prepared for a formidable discussion with Miss Bellamy about two complicated sentences from Richter, which ran thus—

"The cipher of nothing and the circle of perfection have one and the same symbol."

"The white blossom would weep, the red blossom storm, as the pale moon foretells rainy weather, the red moon a tempest (pallida luna pluit, rubicunda flat)."

And no sooner were the cups and saucers removed, than Herr Messing, throwing himself back in his armchair, commenced a luxurious discussion on these two metaphysical problems. Whether Miss Bellamy liked it, I do not know. She resigned herself to the task as patiently as if it were a supreme pleasure, leaving myself and Alfred to our own thoughts.

"You will be glad to hear, Mr. Austin," he commenced, "that it is all right. Hugh received us with some embarrassment, but it gradually melted away, and we spoke as freely as if we had never been estranged. He was rather shy of Elsie, I thought, but she was so watchful and sympathetic and kind, that he was soon at his ease. Do you know, I think his real character has been all the time hidden from us under a hideous mask?"

"I think it quite probable," I said. "I believe most men wear such masks on their faces and their souls, until Death or some supreme calamity tears them off."

"Well, it was a pleasure to see the old Hugh of our boyhood once more. We touched on nothing delicate; but we had a hundred subjects, pleasant enough, to discuss. A load appeared to be lifted off his heart, and he was quite simple and natural. Oh! if he would only live now, how happy we would be!"

"Would it be well?" I asked.

"I don't know," he replied musingly. "We can take but a selfish view of death. We see and acknowledge its beauty : alas ! that the dying cannot see it too ; but it is a *dono infelice della bellezza*, at least to us who are bereft."

There was a pause, and he said—

" It is dangerous to quote Richter in the hearing of the professor; but that is a striking passage where he says, ' On the eye of the spectator, not on him who is struck down, does the battle-axe of death cast a flash of light. It is with the death-bell as with other bells —only he who is afar off, not he who himself stands within the murmuring hemisphere, hears its elevating sounds and tones.' Nevertheless, when I shall hear it toll for poor Hugh, no reasoning can mitigate its accents of bitterness and despair."

"Where will he go," I asked, " after Mayfield is closed ? "

" It is difficult to say. He speaks of Algiers; but I doubt if he has strength to go there."

"And Father Bellamy ? "   .

" Hugh has secured for my poor uncle a quiet chaplaincy in the city. We were more than anxious that both should come to us; but it was not to be."

" Mr. Bellamy will need careful nursing now."

" So we see. And Elsie was most anxious that he should come to us, and spend his last days with us. But no. He has the latent hope of the consumptive, that a warm, dry climate may restore him."

" But he told me he has no hope."

" Nevertheless that nameless buoyancy has cheated him into believing that all is not lost. Yet he has made all preparations for death. See ! "

He took from a desk a new, fresh parchment, marked in red ink the " Last Will and Testament of Hugh Bellamy, M.A." It was perfected that day.

" He leaves everything absolutely to Elsie and me— even the reversion of my uncle's property, which is his."

He folded the parchment and put it back. Then, grasping my hand warmly, he said—

" For this and other countless favours, we have to thank you. God bless you !"

The second evening after, Charlie and I swelled by two units the vast population of London.

If two Thessalian or Thracian Greeks had been suddenly dropped on the granite pavements of Imperial Rome, they could hardly have experienced such vivid and varied experiences as we two young Irishmen, when, for the first time, we were stunned by the noises and blinded by the glare of this Northern Rome. Not that we were quite strangers to its wonderful civilisation, for had we not Piccadilly in miniature in our own Grafton Street ? But everything modern, novel, and wonderful was here accentuated by the multiplicity and variety of objects that met our senses, and overwhelmed them ; and there was the ever-abiding thought, so hateful to us Irishmen, that we stood in the world's metropolis—in the Delphi of the intellectual universe. Everything preached it. The long lines of stately streets, now illuminated by the red reflections of a sunlight that shone through a dim but glorified haze, the asphalted pavements, clean and smooth and polished into an enamelled surface, the odour of cigars in the warm air, the flash of silver and jewellery from the shops, the long, radiant streamers of rich and costly fabrics in the windows, the rattle and noise of cars and omnibuses, the faint tolling of an evening bell, and, above all, the calm, unperturbed look on the olive faces of those young aristocrats, as they stepped from the doors of their clubs, and we could see their spotless evening dress under light surtouts—all proclaimed that we stood in a kingly city, and that these young demigods, who, we knew, would walk to death as calmly as they walked to dinner, were the lords and masters of half the globe. A regiment of soldiers marched by—boys, every one of them—their bugle sounded the formation ; and I could not help thinking that these same boys would, in a few weeks, perhaps, be pelting lead into the naked bodies of some tribe whose records dated back to the time of

Moses, and those bugles would waken echoes in mountain defiles where the face of no white man had yet
been seen.   But let me say these thoughts were mine,
not Charlie's ; for, as we passed along the streets, and
many an eye turned to his girlish face and the long
curls or ringlets that rolled over the collar of his coat,
this curious dialogue took place :—

"We are standing in the world's centre, Charlie."

"Or in the vestibule of hell !"

"The very air is redolent of culture and civilisation !"

"It smells rankly of sin !"

"These are the world's conquerors !"

"Or the devil's slaves !"

"The man who could compel those English to admire
him should be a master and a king !"

"The man they would admire would be rather a
helot and a slave !"

"But all the world's heroes and heroines throng
hither !"

"To be pelted with gold and dismissed with contempt!"

"Well, they are the heirs of all the ages in the fore-
most files of time !"

"Better a Connemara peasant in his rags !"

But when the lamps were lighted, and the streets
put on a new appearance, and the night with its horrors
came down, and the ambassadresses of hell came into
line on the sidewalks, and all the unspeakable iniquity
of the great city appeared to be recognised as part and
parcel of its administration, quite as much as the police,
who looked on with careless eyes, or the legislators,
who passed unheeding to their evening debate, poor
Charlie could stand it no longer; and even I, with all
my new-born admiration, half wished for the quiet
walks at Mayfield, or a whiff of the sea-breezes of Clare.

The night was hot even for June; but it was not
the heat, but the deadly sin-poisoned atmosphere, that
made Charlie throw up his hands with a gesture of
despair, and shriek out—

"I'm choking, Goff! I'm choking!"

We got to a quiet hotel in one of those streets that run down to the river at right angles to the Strand. But even here we could not quite close out the din of the turbulent city. Charlie flung himself on a sofa.

"How long are we condemned to be here?"

"Three weeks at least. So the Grinder said."

He groaned.

"This is a bad preparation for to-morrow, Charlie," I said. "Brace up, man! All our work is before us."

"I am wondering," he replied, "what evil spirit tempted me first to embark on this hateful business. I'm totally unfitted for it. Supposing I should pass, what would I have to do with all these tailor dummies, these mindless apes, we saw this afternoon? How could I get on with them? How sit at their mess-tables, listen to their vapid conversation, exchange weak or ribald jokes with them? And their women-folk? Look here, Goff, can you imagine me in a loose, braided red jacket, spangled like a clown in a circus, with a cigar half burned before me, and a glass of champagne in my hand? It makes myself laugh. And yet mother is looking at me, and telling me to go on; and her heart will break if I fail."

"Charlie," I replied, "to-morrow, after our first bout with the enemy, we will leave this stifling city, and go out to Putney, or somewhere where we shall be within easy reach of the city. But as it is the last three weeks of our life we may spend together, let us make the most of it."

"The last three weeks!" he said, laughing; "what about the Himalayas and Simla?"

"Well, never mind," I replied, as my heart sank. "*Carpe diem!* Let the morrow look for itself."

I took him out of the city to a quiet riverside inn down the river, where we repaid ourselves for the labours and disappointments of the day by glorious morning walks and bathing in the cool river, and, in the evening, such fairy boating and sculling up and

down the broad stream, in pools and shallows, under
leafy coverts, in shy, quiet nooks, and sometimes
in the wake of ocean-bound steamers, that we both
agreed that it was almost as good as Clare, if only
the six hours' daily horror of examination could be
eliminated. For it was with dread and sinking hearts
we slipped in by the morning trains and separated
for our examination—I for Burlington House; Charlie
for some other chamber of torture. After the first
three days we had lost all hope of success. In
my department there were but seventeen vacancies,
and over three hundred candidates; in Charlie's
there were thirty vacancies, and four hundred candidates; and we learned, to our dismay, that most
of these had been up for examination before, and
several were graduates of Oxford and Cambridge Uni-
versities. On Tuesday of the second week, I looked at
my papers, and found, to my horror and dismay, that
very problem in spherical trigonometry which I had
always dreaded and never mastered. The paper swam
before my eyes. I gathered myself together for the
struggle, tried to think of all that I had heard and
learned on the subject. In vain! I could not gather
my wandering thoughts; and when, after the first half
hour, I saw competitor after competitor rising up in
despair, and passing from the examination hall, I flung
down my pen and departed. It was but poor consolation
to know, during the following days, that I had received
the highest marks in French and German—my examiner
being a German, just a counterpart of Herr Messing.
He was most kind; and when he found, to his surprise,
that I knew French and German literature well, it was
no longer an examination, but a quiet and enthusiastic
conversazione which we held. But after my failure in
mathematics I lost heart, and made the usual fatal
blunder of thinking that I had not the ghost of a
chance of success amongst such experts as I saw
around me. Hence I grew careless on such minor subjects as English composition and history; and I touched

only on other questions which with care I might have successfully mastered. To my chagrin and most poignant regret, I ascertained, after the examinations were over, that, with best marks in Latin, Greek, German, and French, and even with fair success in other subjects, I might easily have made up for my failure in mathematics, and reached some one of the coveted places. As a matter of fact, I stood thirty-first on the list, and lost my prize by too much diffidence in myself. Three days after the examination, Charlie received the following courteous reply from the secretary :—

" DEAR SIR,—I regret very much to have to inform you that your name stands 48 in the list of competitors for the vacancies in the Indian Civil Service. Your papers in classics and mathematics were much beyond the average. You failed in modern languages, and your papers in Sanskrit and the native Indian dialects were blank. I have no doubt whatever but that at your next attempt your efforts will be crowned with success. —I have the honour to be, dear sir, yours faithfully,
" EVAN NEPEAN, *Secretary to*
" *Civil Service Commissioners, London.*"

Nothing now remained, after the hideous ordeal, but to pack up our traps and depart. On the pretext of seeing the secretary, Charlie remained in London, having begged me to return to Mayfield. With many misgivings, I consented. He looked so pale and ill, it smote me to the heart to leave him; and the old suspicion, that he was secretly taking drugs or stimulants or sedatives, came back upon me. But we said good-bye at Euston, and he promised to be with me in three days.

CHAPTER XXV

A SAD JOURNEY

ἔνθ᾽ ἄνεμοι πνείουσι δύο κρατεσῆς
ὑπ᾽ ἀνάγκης.
καὶ τύπος ἀντίτυπος, καὶ πῆμ᾽ ἐπὶ
πήματι κεῖται.

" These two winds are ever, by
strong necessity, blowing.
Stroke answers counterstroke, and
evil lies upon evil."

DULL and dispirited, with but a few sanguine thoughts left, and my intense love of learning to buoy me up in this whirlpool of disappointment, I left for Dublin.

"Fate has denied me luck," I thought, "and that fickle jade has given her favours to the stupid, plodding dunces who have crammed their hollow skulls with such memoried learning as will vanish in a week or two. The idiots will strut about in their red cloth and gold lace, and think no more of the gods that have brought them such favours, than the old augurs of the gods whose food they ate.   And I—I—must face poverty— and work, perhaps menially, for a living!"

And yet my thoughts were more for Charlie than myself.   I knew how the dear fellow would feel his rejection.   Proud and sensitive, how could he face home?—his father, whose money he had spent; his mother, whose high ideas of his future were thus rudely shattered; his sister—well, she at least would shield and protect him.   I knew that well.   But what would he do?   And—I started up in the compartment in which we were tearing along at fifty miles an hour towards Holyhead—was I right in leaving him behind me?   If I were asked where he was, what could I say?   Then awful thoughts of what desperate things he might do flashed upon me, and I grew very angry with myself for having listened to his appeals, instead of insisting that he should return with me.   All those terrible " ifs " that make life so unhappy for imaginative people, flashed across me, and I scarcely heeded the steady downpour of rain that washed clean the windows of the carriages, and blurred and blotted out the landscape, and filled the ditches along the line of rail with pools of brown water, and made a winter landscape where summer should have been smiling. We were bowling along at an even rate of speed, when suddenly the train was checked, and we came to a full stop, in the midst of a desolate plain between Rugby and Chester. This was annoying enough, for if we delayed, we should hardly catch the mail-boat at Holyhead; but our annoyance gave way to gratitude, when we ascertained that the line in front was completely swept away by the flood—ballast, sleepers, and all—leaving the rails for a space of twelve to twenty feet hanging naked over an abyss of swirling waters. Had we not been warned— and this, too, was fortuitous, but providential—we should have dashed into this chasm, at a tremendous rate of speed, and been wrecked without a possibility of escape. What was to be done ? We had to wait some dreary hours until the up mail to London arrived at the opposite side. Then planks were flung across the waters, and the passengers and mails transferred from one train to the other. As I stepped gingerly enough along the trembling board, I lifted my eyes to see—the Grinder [crossing within two feet of me. He was picking his steps carefully, owing to his weak sight. In a moment a thousand ideas ran through my mind. Would I speak to him ? Would he recognise me ? How would he take it ? Meanwhile the stream of passengers was pushing us in opposite directions; but I could not help shouting—

"Mr. Bellamy!"

He appeared to take no notice, or my voice was drowned in the noise of the waters; but when I stood on firm ground again, I looked back and saw him peering curiously across the line. Then, as if disappointed, he turned away, and I saw him enter a third-class carriage. I never saw him again. Disappointment and despair in this poor soul, too, I conjectured. With all his worldly wisdom and his contempt for sentiment, he was another stray fragment amongst the flotsam and jetsam of wrecked souls.

Three days afterwards, when I called for the last time at Mayfield, to gather up my books and other trifling possessions, a letter was put into my hand, with the postmark " Ennis." With some evil foreboding in my mind, I broke the seal, and read :—

" DEAR MR. AUSTIN,—Have you any news of Charlie ? Did he accompany you to Ireland ? We are distracted with fear and apprehension. Tell him, if he is with you, to return home at once. There is nothing to forgive. We shall only be too glad to have him home again. Let him return immediately ; and come with him, if you can.—Yours faithfully,

" MARY TRAVERS."

Here were my worst fears realised ! And what should I say ? How could I face his friends with the assurance that I had left him alone in London, in weak health and dispirited.

It was no time for reflection—it was a time for action. At first, I determined to run across to London and bring Charlie home with me, irksome and trouble-some as the journey might be. But then, perhaps he had already returned to Ireland, and I should have gone on a wild-goose chase. Clearly the first thing to be done was to ascertain if he had come back ; but how ? I was at my wits' end. I went straight to the North Wall booking-office and made most minute inquiries of the porters there. They could give no information. I rushed back to Kingsbridge terminus. Official after official repeated my hue-and-cry description : A young man, about 18, fair-haired, blue eyes, tall and straight, and—

" Gentlemanly looking ? "

" Yes," I said enthusiastically ; " very much so."

" We haven't seen him. Try booking-office."

I tried booking-office. The clerk nibbled his pencil, swept and scraped his memory, to no avail. Couldn't remember any such person. I turned away in despair; and I must have looked very miserable, for a voice at my elbow said—

"Dead broke?"

I turned angrily, and saw a young fellow, gaudily dressed, fashionable from the hat and flashy necktie down to—not his boots; no, they were patched and broken—a sure sign of faded gentility. But, as I turned, his manner changed into a confidential swagger.

"I beg pardon. I am peculiarly circumstanced. Hold cheque on Hibernian Bank, value £10. Bank just closed. Am on my way to south to my relations. Could you accommodate me with a pound, just to pay my train-fare, and I leave you the cheque as security?"

I could hardly help smiling at the fellow's impudence; but I answered cheerily—

"Am sorry, old man. Pounds are not like pebbles with me just now."

"Just so," said he. "Dead broke, as I thought. But lend a hand, just to give a fellow a drink. I haven't tasted a drop since a fellow-student, like ourselves, lent me a hand yesterday."

"Where was he going?" I said listlessly.

"To Queenstown. Plucked in London. Ashamed to go home. Bound for the land of the free and the brave"—

"Look here," said I, holding him by the collar; "tell me what he was like, and I'll give you as much as you can drink for a month."

"You're a brick," said he; "but, meanwhile, I should prefer my liberty. I'm a free citizen, even in this downtrodden country."

"All right," said I, unhanding him. "But, hang it, man, can't you make allowance for a friend's impatience?"

"Yes, if you were a friend," said he suspiciously; "but what if you were a cop, or one of Mallon's men? I'd see you and your month's drink in—well, in the Liffey before I'd tell you anything."

I was turning away disgusted, when he laid his hand on my arm.

"No, you're not a detective, I see," said he; "and I'll tell you all. What was this fair-haired Norwegian from the land of the Sagas like? He was tall, and pink and white, like a consumptive milliner, and, as the novels say, he had a far-off look in his eyes—altogether he was a *fin-de-siècle* young man; and he wore a pea-jacket, grey trousers, flannel tennis shirt, turned-down collar, and a spanking tie that went floating away into space. Honestly, as a fellow-student, and as one, perhaps, that had paid his addresses to Calliope, I pitied him, and—he pitied me. 'Non ignara mali, miseris succurrere disco.' Dear old Dido!"

"But now," said I, humouring him, "you know so much, you can tell me more. Has he sailed?"

"Do you take me for a Mahatma," said he, "or a Theosophist, that I could see or sail through space? Nevertheless, reason supplies the place of bilocation. No! He has not sailed. He will sail to-morrow (Sunday), by the *Servia*, or the *Germanic*, or the *City of Berlin*."

"Could I reach Queenstown in time?"

"Certainly. Train at 3 P.M. Queenstown, 10 P.M. Visit lodging-houses. Agencies all shut. And if you're stranded, ask for Kelly, amateur detective, friend of mine. He'll help you. And now"—as I handed him a half-crown—"*au revoir, et au reçevoir*, as we used to say in France."

I called him back. He came, leisurely biting a straw.

"What's your name?"

"*N'importe*," said he; "call me Nimrod."

Two miserable hours passed by, during which I studied impatiently the bills and advertisements at the station, until D. W. D. swam before my eyes, and Lafayette's wonderful pictures lost all attraction. I made a hasty dinner on a sandwich and a cup of coffee, and at last found myself in a third-class compartment, speeding rapidly southward. I pulled out a pocket

copy of *The Tempest;* and with my own dreams, and
those of the great master, I forgot for a time my
troubles, and passed heedlessly from station to station.
Then this wretched mind of mine, undisciplined by
philosophy and untaught by experience, would build up
ghastly castles of contingent misfortunes, until poverty,
disgrace, disappointment, and a possible future like
Nimrod's, rose in hideous possibilities before me. It
was a decided relief when, under a gentle twilight, and
with all God's stars glittering in pale blue skies, I
entered Queenstown. It was late, yet I could not defer
my search until morning. The most expeditious way
to carry it out was to seek Kelly. I found him, without
much trouble, in the third-class refreshment room, a
glass of ale before him, and a portentous cigar in his
mouth. I made known my business. He received the
communication with the dignity of a Comanche warrior,
looking me all over at the time, and studying his own
portrait in a huge mirror—a proceeding that appeared
to give him intense satisfaction. Then, after inviting
me by a gesture to partake of his hospitalities, which I
declined, he finished his libations, and, shaking himself
together, he said laconically, "Come."

Without a word he led me through the gas-lit
streets. Even at this late hour, groups of emigrants
were standing and chatting around the doors of the
lodging-houses, from which came sounds of violins or
concertinas, and the rapid pattering of feet on the
boards—a certain sign that our exiles were trying to
chase away regrets for the past, or misgivings about the
future, by the songs and dances of the motherland,
which they were soon to forget. A warm, salt vapour
crept in from the sea, which, now at high tide, reached
to the level of the quays; and we could see, under the
faint aurora of the skies, the blue-black waters heaving
and tossing lazily under the tidal influence and the
occasional disturbance of a passing boat. A cross-
channel steamer coming down the channel opposite
Spike Island made itself visible only by the headlight

and the faint reflection of its cabin windows, whilst the
quiet churning of its screw, at less than half-speed,
scarcely drove a faint ripple to the camber, where fishing
lighters, with quite a little forest of masts, swayed and
rolled uneasily.   Here and there a ship captain, smoking
a fragrant cigar, chatted with the merchants of the
Beach ; and pilots, with peaked caps and blue cloth coats
shining with brass buttons, waited for an order, when the
ship captains, tired of the hospitalities on shore, would
make up their minds to heave anchor for Falmouth or
London.   The lights on Haulbowline and Spike glittered
and shone in a straight line, and, far away across the
bay, Whitegate showed its tiny illuminations, broken
sometimes by the black hulks of wheat-ships lying in
the man-of-war roads   My detective, silent and im-
perturbable, made a few laconic inquiries at the houses
on the Beach, and scarcely manifested any interest in
the matter until we came to the Bench, a broad square
at the end of the main street, and opening into what is
known as the Holy Ground.   Here, too, we were doomed
to disappointment, until at last the hesitating answers
of a lodging-house keeper aroused suspicions, which
were verified ; when at last Kelly quietly said—

" Your friend is here.   Now, do you wish to see him
at once, or will you wait till morning ? "

" I'll see him at once," I said.   " You need only
mention my name, Goff Austin, and he'll see me."

The two men exchanged meaning glances ; and the
lodging-house keeper, calling a girl, bade her go upstairs and see if " that young gent had gone to
bed."

Apparently he had not.   Kelly lazily taking the
cigar from his mouth, whispered to me—

" I think you had better wait till morning.   He can't
go without your knowledge."

These proceedings excited all kinds of foolish suspicions
in my mind, and I said determinedly—

" I insist on seeing Mr. Travers at once.   Show me
where he is."

The girl, at a nod from her master, took up a light, and ascended a flight of steps, rough with dirt and the accumulated lees of porter; and on the first landing she pushed open a door, placed the candle on a dresser, and, closing the door gently, passed downstairs. When my eyes became accustomed to the room, I saw I was in a wretched back bedroom, whose solitary window opened on a short yard, walled in by a perpendicular cliff. There was a wretched bed in one corner, a round table in the centre, and there, leaning heavily on his outstretched arm, which enclosed a filthy measure of halfdrained porter, and with one of his yellow locks dabbling in the same filthy fluid, was my idol, my heart's dearest friend, the one who had always touched my highest ideals, my paragon, my saint—drunk!

I fastened the door, and sat down upon the bed. "Oh! Charlie, Charlie, is this the culmination of all our hopes, the realisation of all our dreams? What airy castles we used to build on those summer evenings, under the fragrant limes and the whispering beeches! You were to be, you remember, a high official in India, with K.C.M.G. to your honoured name; and some day, as Commissary, I was to visit you in Simla or Benares, and you would come forth from your Indian palace and welcome me, and I should see your fair English wife and children; and a host of black servants would do your every bidding; and in the sight of the Himalayan snows we would smoke and chat, whilst the neverceasing punkah tempered the Indian heat, and all our thoughts would go back to Mayfield, and, grey and bronzed, we would laugh at the escapades of our studentlife, and conjecture what had become of our less fortunate companions; and then we should look forward to a life of ease and honour at home—grey, wrinkled veterans, who had done our duty, and were now retired on handsome pensions—and the whole picture was gay with sunshine, and the laughter of our rose-strewn lives." He turned uneasily and looked around. His face was flushed, and his bloodshot eyes did not see me. He mumbled something, then fell into his stupor again. I leaned my face on my hands, and let the burning tears roll silently through my fingers.

———

CHAPTER XXVI

THE PARTING OF THE WAYS

"I said, let my body dwell in poverty, and my hands be as the hands of the toiler; but let my soul be as a temple of remembrance, where the treasures of knowledge enter, and the inner sanctuary is hope. I know what I chose. They said, 'He feeds himself on visions,' and I denied not; for visions are the creators and feeders of the world. I see, I measure the world as it is, which the vision will create anew."—G. ELIOT.

THE bell for vespers was sending its deep tones far and wide over vibrating waters the next evening, as Charlie and I stood under the shadow of the great Southern Cathedral. The level sun was striking glints of light from every tiny mica leaf in the grey granite, and pouring quite a flood of yellow splendour through the great rose-window in the western gable. The high, fair building looked so light and airy in its latticework and fretwork of granite and limestone, that it was almost a shock to touch it, and feel the cold, hard, irresponsive texture, which seemed to say, "I am for eternity, friend: you are an ephemera." We took our seats far up the aisle, and in sight of a wretched organ, which threw its hazy notes hardly to where we were sitting. Then commenced the beautiful Evening Service of Compline, which a late cardinal used to recommend as the best form of evening prayer for Catholic families. The old notes, familiar to the sweet singers of David's time, came to us in the tiny trebles of children's voices; and there was something very sweet and pathetic about it all; but, alas! let me confess it, it was all as unintelligible to us Catholic students as if chanted in

Arabic to some Oriental monotone. In sheer weariness of spirit, Charlie took up a coverless, ragged primer of devotion that lay upon the bench, and he soon became absorbed in it. I studied the stained-glass window in the apse, the attitude of the priest, the restlessness of the acolytes, a bird that went bobbing up and down on a lady's bonnet in front; and I thought of the awful solicitude of a bald-headed man before me to keep intact the thread of grey hairs which he had brought up from one ear, and had spread with infinite care across the shining expanses of the occiput. Then I thought that Charlie was unusually and abnormally interested in this tattered leaflet; I thought I saw a tear glisten in his eye and break upon his hand. But I said nothing. When Benediction commenced, he handed me the booklet, and I read—

"He that dwelleth in the aid of the Most High, shall abide under the protection of the God of Jacob.

"He shall say to the Lord: Thou art my protector, and my refuge: my God, in Him will I trust.

"For He hath delivered me from the snare of the hunters: and from the sharp word.

"He will overshadow thee with His shoulders: and under His wings thou shalt trust.

"His truth shall compass thee with a shield: thou shalt not be afraid of the terror of the night.

"Of the arrow that flieth in the day, of the business that walketh about in the dark: of invasion, or of the noonday devil.

"A thousand shall fall at thy side, and ten thousand at thy right hand: but it shall not come nigh thee.

"There shall no evil come to thee: nor shall the scourge come near thy dwelling.

"For He hath given His angels charge over thee: to keep thee in all thy ways.

"In their hands they shall bear thee up: lest thou dash thy foot against a stone.

"Thoushalt walk upon the asp and the basilisk: and thou shalt trample under foot the lion and the dragon.

"Because he hoped in Me I will deliver him: I will protect him because he hath known My name.

"He shall cry to Me, and I will hear him: I am with him in tribulation, I will deliver him, and glorify him.

"I will fill him with length of days; and I will show him My Salvation."

I pondered long and earnestly over these words; but, alas! the demon of intellectual pride was at my side, and he whispered: "Songs of the world's childhood! scraps of Hebrew poetry! What are they, crude and simple, to the majestic sweep of your Homer, or the resonant cadences of Virgil? And their philosophy! Well, Seneca has said equally good things, and taught you that man, to succeed, must rest upon himself alone!" I returned the torn leaves to Charlie, but, happily, without my doubts. And as the last strains of the "Laudate" echoed through the incense-laden air, we stood up to depart. Charlie lingered behind me as we passed down through the aisle. He was watching the faces of the people, as they still knelt at their devotions. Old women, scarred and wrinkled from their battles with the years; young girls, fresh and fair and pure; old men, battered by many a storm at sea and many a rough stand-up fight with poverty at home; and ruddy, bronzed young men, with uplifted faces and fearless eyes, as if they were ever looking at death, and never blenched before him; and on all an expression of rapt devotion, of abstraction from this world's wretched affairs, such as Giotto or Angelico, with their beautiful, poetic, mediæval faith, gave their nimbus-crowned Virgins and apostles. Charlie lingered long about that church and its worshippers, as if he wished that the peace and devotion that filled its sacred aisles might steal into his heart, and remain there. At last, in response to a gesture of impatience on my part, he came out with a preoccupied air, and leaned on the wall that overhung the row of dingy cottages named the Rock. For a long time, in silence he continued to gaze out over the bright expanse of waters, as if he were solving, by communing with Nature, some intricate problem that was puzzling him. At last, with a sigh, he turned, and said—

"Goff, to what religion do we belong?"

I smiled at the naïveté of the question, and said—

"I suppose we're some kind of Roman Catholics."

"Because," said he, in a musing voice, "if we had, or rather if I had had half the faith and devotion of these simple people, you would never have found me degraded and disgraced as you found me last night"—

"Don't speak cf it, Charlie," said I gently; but he interrupted me fiercely.

"Speak of it!" said he, and there was quite an unwonted look in his eyes—"speak of it! I shall never cease to *think* of it, which is worse, until God calls me, and tells me with His own lips that I am forgiven."

He was again silent.

"Do you remember," he continued, after a pause, "those branded marks with which criminals and deserters are seared—big, big D's marked on the breast, or between the shoulders, and which, however faded by time, will start forth red and angry if you touch or irritate the flesh? Well, such a brand shall I carry to my grave."

"Oh, now, Charlie," said I, "this won't do. You are taking an accident for a crime. This is a morbid condition of mind, which you must shake off at once."

"If," said Charlie, not heeding what I was saying, but musing to himself as before—"if in these so-called high-class colleges they taught us a little more of Christianity and a little less of paganism, a little more of Christian mysteries and a little less of the worship of Isis and Osiris, a little more of God's Mother and a little less of Minerva and Aphrodite, perhaps you and I would be better equipped for the battle of life, in which we have just sustained our first fall. It is not right to be vindictive, but I cannot help a feeling of con-

temptuous anger against the men to whom our educa‧
tion was committed "—

He paused, and continued looking steadily to the
horizon.   Then, in the same musing tone, he resumed—
"Well, I have got my life-lesson, Goff!   *Woe to those
who have kept from us the corn and wine of life, and left
us the husks and the lees !* "

It has often surprised me during life, with what
lightning-like rapidity such delicate feminine souls rush
to safe conclusions with unerring intuition.   Here this
young lad had struck a primal truth which I discovered
only after many years, and untold sufferings and
humiliations.   I was so far from recognising then the
paramount necessity of religion as the basis of all that
is true and noble and desirable in life, that just at this
moment I was soliloquising mentally—

"Poor fellow! he has not my vast reserve of intellectual and mental pabulum to fall back upon.   Why,
come what will, so long as I have my books, I shall be
satisfied to live on bread and milk at five cents a day,
and polish lenses like Spinoza!"

And with that magnificent *aplomb* which I would then
have called the superb energies of a young divinity who
had for the first time heard the morning stars sing to
each other, but which I would call now the placid self-
sufficiency of a callow youth, ignorant of life, its issues
and its tragedies, I looked fearlessly into the future,
and went back to our wretched lodgings humming the
Marching-song of Goethe—

> " The Future hides in it
> Gladness and sorrow,
> We press still thorough,
> Nought that abides in it
> Daunting us—onward ! "

THE END
(is not yet)

www.ingramcontent.com/pod-product-compliance
Lightning Source LLC
Chambersburg PA
CBHW030325270326
41926CB00010B/1509